Reprogram Your Mind for Success and Happiness

Reprogram Your Mind for Success and Happiness

A Step-by-Step Guide to Becoming Physically, Financially, and Spiritually Successful

Cleophus Jackson

iUniverse, Inc.
Bloomington

Reprogram Your Mind for Success and Happiness
A Step-by-Step Guide to Becoming Physically, Financially, and Spiritually Successful

iUniverse books may be ordered through booksellers or by contacting:

iUniverse
1663 Liberty Drive
Bloomington, IN 47403
www.iuniverse.com
1-800-Authors (1-800-288-4677)

ISBN: 978-1-4620-3142-9 (sc)
ISBN: 978-1-4502-9250-4 (hc)
ISBN: 978-1-4620-3143-6 (ebk)

Printed in the United States of America

iUniverse rev. date: 09/09/2011

CONTENTS

PREFACE

Oh Heavenly and Most Gracious Father,
I pray each and every day that you will guide me so that I
want stand in my own way. And that you will give me the
wisdom to know when to hold on or when to let go and
make the right decision with grace.
I pray that you will allow this work to give back hope to
those who have none. Let every eye whether closed or open
know that your light shine on the poor as well as the rich.

AMEN.

I was born poor in a small town in Mississippi called Alligator. Neither
my father nor real mother raise me. That job was left up to my step
grandmother, (if there is such a name) but my older brother and I called
her mama. Mama was already in her sixty when I was born. She didn't
believe in boys taking a bath but once a month. We only had two pairs of
pants for each school year. There were never tooth brushes, soap, or combs
in the house until we were senior in high school. The electricity to the
house never stayed on after dark not even during the summer months.

When we finish high school we could not attend the graduation, because we
did not own a vehicle nor could we afford to pay anyone for transportation.
Not having money to afford nothing but the basic necessities to sustain
life as we grew up, caused my brother and I many days of embarrassments,
harassment and a terrible inferiority complexion. Believe me when I tell
you that if I can be successful, then anyone can.

I could tell you over and over again that you too can be the man or woman that you would like to be, but I would like to do more. In this book I will show you how to become successful. All that is require from you is to purchase this book and read it with an open mind. If you are already successful and feel that you do not need anymore motivation in your life then pass this book or another one like it as a gift to a friend or family member.

Everyone wants to know the secret to success. Most people already process the knowledge or know the secret, the problem isn't not knowing, the problem is believing. If you can convince your mind and turn it into a believable, you will become successful. This universe will open up and provide for you, all you need to bring to the table is to believe and have the will.

INTRODUCTION

Are you wondering what tomorrow will bring? With so much going wrong in the world today, weather like we never seen before, terrorists, abroad and home grown, housing and stock markets turned upside down, wars, crimes and unemployment at an all time high. Just what can we count on for sure? You can count on seen more of the same. And if this is not enough to just make you want to raise both hands up in the air, try this one for size. The United States is not the king of economic that she once was. China and Japan are moving faster and faster at becoming an economy giant. Now historically speaking the economy follow a certain pattern prosperity, recession, depression and recovery. With gas prices sky rocking something got to give. We are moving fast to a world where one job in a normal family of three will not put enough food on the table and still pay the bill, not to mention higher learning.

Most people hate the one job that they have, now imagine having two jobs that you hate. Excuse me for that, now let me come back down to earth. The average person right now is happy that he or she have a job. All of us know somebody if not us, then someone close to the family or a friend that do not have a job and have been unemployed for some time now. The days of staying at one job for twenty, thirty or forty years are gone. Everyday you go to work with this thought on your mind—is this going to be my last day? Those of us who do have jobs are not going to work everyday because we want to, but because we have to, period. Ask most people, wouldn't it be nice to work less and earn more?

Why yes of course they would say, but how or what can I do? On the other hand, there are others out there who put in forty plus hours every week but with unlimited taxes they're so busy trying to make a living that they don't have time to make any money. The good news for those of you who ask-what can you do is that this reality doesn't have to be yours unless you choose it.

This book is about becoming successful, anybody can be successful. There are a few people out there who are doing just that. But it not easy. Some years ago someone did a study of one hundred men starting from the time they finish high school until they were around sixty-five years old. The day they all graduated from high school, everyone of them had high hopes for the future. They were wide eyed, walking with a swagger couldn't wait to take on life challenges. By the time they reached sixty-five only five of them has become successful. What happen to all of that ambitions they all had after finishing high school? How can you be born and grow up in the richest country in the world and not be successful. It is easy folks, it is called life. Life is a battle for territory, "you much fight for what you want out of life". "The day you stop fighting for what you want, out of life, life will give you what you don't want."

Successful people are wired, they are abnormal because they account for about ten percent of the population. They have a drive in them that separate them from the so-called norm. While everyone else is complaint about their jobs or not having one, these successful-wired mined people are enjoying and rising to the top position in their respected fields. While ninety percent of the population is working one or more jobs that they hate, or don't have a job, these successful-wired minded people are self-employed and financial free. So my question to you, are they abnormal because they do the things that make them successful? For those of you who are working at one or more jobs that you hate or do not have a job at all, this book may be for you. I say may be for you because a book is just a tool, it is only good for the purpose for which it is being used. It can help the so called normal individual become a high achiever. I guarantee that no matter what dollar amount you paid for this book if used properly it will be worth a hundred times even thousand times more.

LIVE YOUR DREAMS

What if I told you that you can attain anything that this world had to offer? What if I told you that through faith anything including moving mountains is possible? One of the things that astonished me the most about life is people. Most people in the world have no self-realization. Most of us have heard someone says that "you can be anything that you want". We ourselves may have told a friend or family member the same thing. The question is when you hear or say it do you believe it? I've found that ninety percents of the people that I have met do not believe this; so they are normal, but there is that ten percent of wired individuals or the so called abnormal who do believe that God makes every thing possible for them. This is the main reason why they are successful and others are not. There are people who go to church faithfully every Sunday and sometimes doing the week, yet most of the faithful are struggling through life. Some have unhappy marriages, living from one pay check to the next one.

If you haven't to be one of these faithful, don't you think its time you re-check your faith? What God are you serving? I believe that if my earthly father was rich in money, I being his son could go to him and if nothing else I could borrow enough money to get me going in the right direction. I believe this whole hardly because I am my father son and he would want for me as much as he wants for himself. Most of you that know your father knows that if he was in that position that you could attain from him some of his richest. If you can believe this about your earthy father surely you know that your heavenly father who is trillions times greater, who made the world and everything in it, including you, knows your wants as well as your needs. All you have to do is ask and it shall be giving unto you. Knock and the door share be open unto you. Seek and you shall find.

For everyone who asks will receive, and anyone who seeks will find, and the door will be opened to him who knocks. Would any of you who are fathers give your son a stone when he asks for bread? Or would you give him a snake when he asks for a fish?

As bad as you are, you know how to give good things to your children. How much more then, will your Father in heaven give good things to those who ask him! Matthew 7, 7-11 and Luke 11, 9-13. This is not just lip services, this is the way that we are suppose to pray, and believe that we will receive what ever we ask of our Heavenly Father. So my concluding is that the reason why many of you are in the shape that you are in today with all of your church going, praising and shouting that you do is that you don't believe in the God that you serve. For the Lord said "if ye had faith as a grain of mustard seed, ye might say unto this sycamore tree, be thou plucked up by the root, and be thou planted in the sea; and it should obey you. Luke 17:6. You will hear me say this time and time again; even thou we didn't have anything to do with being born into this world, but our Father in Heaven loved us so much that he gave us a gift and a tool box. The tool box is for us to fix or work on the gift so that we can best serve God, for it come with many manuals and instructions. And if we don't know what our gift is, it is a guide or road map for us to follow to help us find our gift. When I need help understanding something or others, I always turn to the bible that I consider my toolbox, here is a sample of what it offer;

"THE WAY OF SALVATION"
"COMFORT IN TIME OF LONELINESS"
"COMFORT IN TIME OF SORROW"
"RELIEF IN TIME OF SUFFERING"
"GUIDANCE IN TIME OF DECISION"
"PROTECTION IN TIME OF DANGER"
"COURAGE IN TIME OF FEAR"
"PEACE IN TIME OF TURMOIL"
"REST IN TIME OF WEARINESS"
"STRENGTH IN TIME OF TEMPTATION"
"WARNING IN TIME OF INDIFFERENCE"
"FORGIVENESS IN TIME OF CONVICTION".

The God that I served is all things and his power is immeasurable. Who else could make a covenant with a ninety-nine years old man and bless his wife at ninety years old to bare a child? I don't know if you are religious or not, but in these times especially now, it help to believe in something a little higher than you are. For the first time in the United States of America we have a black president. This could not have happen if not for the will of God. There are many things that I do not know but one thing for sure is tomorrow is not promise to you. If you don't follow your dream today then when? If you have not set down and talk to yourself about what it is you want out of life, then ask yourself, why not? Have you ever dreamed or played the game of make believe? I think where the two different is that make believe is controlled by the conscious, and dreams are controlled by the subconscious. Make believe or imaginations are moved by emotions that go off on self-inspired tours.

Trying not to confuse you so just remember this key thing, anything that's controlled by our conscious is limited where ability is concern. Then there are dreams that had no limitation. The key point here is that anything that is controlled by the subconscious is closer to infinite intelligence. Anything where God is concern had no limitation. You are reading this and you're properly wondering where I am going with all of this. I am talking about your dreams. Some years ago a study was conducted on some people concerning dreams. These people went to sleep but when ever they started to dream they were awaking. Most of them got over eight hours of sleep but because they were not allowed to dream they became very disoriented, irritable and perturbed. Dreams are important. In order to get a good night rest you much dream.

We all dream, not only doing the night but dreams doing our waking hours are important too. The dreams that we have when we are asleep are the ones with unlimited boundaries. They are so powerful that obstacles becomes opportunities. There are no end. The characters are illusion yet the reactions are real. At some point in your life you have had what we call a wet dream. The feeling of ecstatic as a result of our dreams. Why you are mentally dreaming your body is going through all of the changes as if it was the real thing. For example, out blood pressure changes, heart beats a little faster. If you are a male you will have an erection. And if you are a female your nippers will harden. While you are asleep and dreaming the dream is real. The only way that you find out that it's not real is to wake up.

Have you ever dream about having lots of money only to awaken the same broke person you were when you laid down? Doing the dreaming phase, the money was so real, you could feel or smell it. What if you could bring on anyone dream or imagination of your choosing, whenever you wanted to? I hate to disappoint you, but you can. Anything that you wish to improve upon, change or accomplish in this world just set the precise image in your mind before going to bed. You should also practice this several times throughout the day. The thing that you want to make sure of is that you are setting a positive image. For example if you want to loose weight, then see yourself having already lost the desired amount of weights.

WHAT THE MIND CAN CONCEIVE, THE BODY CAN ACHIEVE.

No matter how good our intentions are, what we would like to accomplish in life, there are some obstacles or forces that tried to stop us from being all that we could be. Life can be treacherous, sometimes down right nasty. There are times when the only thing that holding you back from becoming the man or woman that you would like to be is the man or woman in the mirror. The mind, our mind, a force within a force. So powerful that ninety-nine point nine percent of us only use approximately five percent of it. Yet God gave us power over our own mind, but many of us don't believe it or know how to tap into this perpetual gold mine. When it come to the mind there are some dysfunctions that many of us have as individuals that we much overcome in order to become successful at anything. I called these dysfunction enemies of the mind. Some of them are LOW SELF-ESTEEM, LOW SELF-CONFIDENCE, LACK OF MOTIVATION and PROCRASTINATION. Before we talk about low self-esteem, let's talk about self-esteem period.

What is self-esteem? SELF-ESTEEM is a tangible or visible representation of oneself. Most importantly, it is the way you see yourself. SELF-ESTEEM had a lot to do with an ideal. This ideal is based on your self-image. What ever you tell yourself, the mind will believe. If you tell yourself that you are bad or poor in reading continually, the mind will start to believe and will perform accordingly. To get anywhere successfully in life you much believe in yourself. A man or woman who do not believe in self or see themselves in a negative way have already failed the first law of success. Your self-esteem can be programmed for you by your love ones, friends or others. They can either cause you to have low self-esteem or high self-esteem. Often times your mind will be programed in a negative way instead of a positive way. Let me give you an example; I have a friend, his name is mike. When mike was just a child, his parents would always feed him with statements such as the following:

"You are stupid",

"You are no good",

"Nobody wants you" and

"You will never amount to anything".

These statements are called enforcements. After awhile mike starts to believe what his parents was telling him about himself. So whenever he made a mistake he would say something like I'm just stupid or I'm no good. Even if he didn't say it out aloud, just to think it, they are then called reinforcements. I would like to think that no-one intentionally would tell someone that they love these types of negative things. But life being reality, it does happen, more often then we know. Make sure that you don't be like mike parents. But on the other hands if you are on the receiving end of these negative statements, then you much immediately began some type of treatment; to re-wire or reprogram yourself. If your self-esteem is in anyway damages where you don't like your self or think you're not as good as the next person you must get some help. In some cases a little self help is all that's required. Then there are other cases that require a professional. It seen funny if not ironic that low or high self-esteem is a result of how other people treated you in life. As I said early in this chapter your parents, siblings, even your superiors, peers and other significant people have shaped your self-esteem for you. Through their psychological messages you have determined your worth.

More often people with low self-esteem have been lied to. Instead of positive reinforcement some one gave you negative ones. Then you grew up believing that you are worthless. This is not true, but you end up believing it anyway. Most people with low self-esteem see themselves in an unduly and negative way. But they view others in an unduly positive way. Now that you know all of this; let's fix this problem and hope that it will last forever. None of us are perfect. Every human on this earth has faults, problems and some misgiving about something that's going on in their life. Treat yourself with respect: behave the way you would like people to treat treat you. Believe in yourself.

Loving yourself is the first step in believing in self. You must believe that you are special for this time and place you were put here o n this earth for a reason. You much believe that if someone else can do great thing-so can you. Don't accept put down or allow others to make you feel bad. It been said that misery love company that is universal true. No one control how you think or feel but you. No matter what someone said it still up to you as to how you are going to—receive this, make you feel or how you are going to response to it. Stop looking at just the bad things in your life. You are important and everyone in this world is good at somethings and is bad at others. We are all weak in some area or another. Rather then focusing on how bad you are why not focus on improving some of the things that you know you are good at.

I once heard someone say "I don't have any friends". Well let's take a closer look at the word friend. You know there are two types. One is called associated friend: someone you like to hang out with because they are so cool, going to the mall, playing some sort of sports. Someone you like to talk to every now and then. While they are in your present you are the best thing since slice bread; but boy, behind your back you are worthless. On the other hand you have a true friend: This person make you angry at time because he or she speaks the truth about you to you. No matter what time day or night they are willing to lend you a helping hand.

You keep hurting their feeling or letting them down times and times again but yet they are still around. In short a true friend will be with you to the end no matter what you do. If you are like most people you would rather have a true friends. They are hard to come by because they give it to you straight. If you have one in your life, you are blessed. So don't feel bad, now that you know what true friendship is; be a true friend to your self first, and you just might find that you;re all the friend you may need. Don't spend time with people who mistreat you for no reason at all.

Find people who give you recognition and just make you feel good to be around them.

I told you early that misery love company. Most of the times when people say something to make you feel bad is because they themselves are suffering from low self-esteem and are trying to take it out on you. If they can make you feel bad then they feel good because they have accomplished their goal of not feeling bad all by themselves. Remember you are important there isn't but one of you and no-one on this earth is exactly like you. If you are feeling kind of special, "great because you are".

MOTIVATION

This is one of my favorite subjects, because without it, success isn't the only thing you will not achieve. A lack of motivation could be the determining factor in failure.

MOTIVATION: Is a powerful emotion that inspires and inculcates aspiration and values. Concerned with an individual's representation of his or her environment as a determinism of how he or she strives for achievement. Motivation is the get up and go of any goal, mission or your willingness to succeed. Frustrations can be an important comportment of motivation. Simple put, you must become angry at your approach to success if what you are doing is not working. This is more on the line of negative emotions, but you must be able to view this in a different light and start using them to get ahead, if you tell yourself what I am doing is not working then you need to find a better way.

HIGH ACHIEVERS: Most high achievers say that you must condition your mind to focus on what you are capable of. The more of your abilities you can tap into the better you will see your self capable of doing. Reviewing previous successes is a powerful way to shift how you think and feel. Surround your work area with evidence of your previous successes. Place certificate, awards and photos in a prominent location. Keep letters and newspaper clipping that highlight your achievements. When you remind yourself of what you are capable of, you will naturally start to demand more of yourself and you'll feel inspired to achieve greater results. You may think that these high achievers intuitively knows how to get motivated. But that is not the case most had to learn motivation techniques, which anyone can learn. These skills are developed through a need or desire to make one dream come true. Let's look at some of these techniques. Remember that the more you use them the successful you will become and through the eyes of others the wired you will be.

1. Set goals, write them down on paper , put a date on it, identify the obstacles, identify the people you need to work with, develop a plain of action and find out what in it for you.
2. Change your habits, if you want to see where you will be one year from now, just look back at what you were doing one year ago, change your habits, change your life.
3. Surround yourself with motivated, people. Remember birds of a feather flied together.
4. Take risks, seek more responsibility. A man who risk nothing, gain nothing.
5. Stop being afraid of failing; the fear of failure will keep you from success. Failure is only a by-product of creativity that challenges you to take risks and teaches you to keep trying until you get it right. Fail your way to success.
6. You must have vision; without vision other forces control your life. Your life and destiny should be yours and yours along to control. Success come from visualizing yourself the way you want to be. The real question is how do you see yourself? When you look in the mirror, the you , you see is the you, you'll be,
7. Share with other your appreciation for living. Share the power, glory and the motivation you learned; for it will continue to grow.

Our wishes, wants, and most importantly our needs constitute motivation, this is the driving force that impels us to act and directs our behavior toward a worth while goal. We all share certain motivations, but according to particular personal and our social situations, motivations can vary in its importance.

PROCRASTINATIION

"Beginning is works half done-every beginner is a winner".

If time is important to you, then let me introduce to you an enemy of time; I call him Mr. Procrastination, better known as the thief of time. Oh yea if you have the inability to get things done. Or if you just like to put things off until tomorrow, and for some unexplained reason you just can't seen to ever finish things that you started; I say to you welcome to the procrastinating club. Does not cost much to join, just set right where ever you are and do nothing and I guarantee you a special spot with millions of other unsuccessful people. But if you are reading this then I will bet the bank that you don;t want to continue to be a member of this club. First you must realize that procrastination is a psychological problem. There is no single cause nor is their single cure. Some causes are phobia, depression, low self-esteem, bad time management, self-sabotage, bad decision making or lack of motivation issues. All of these factors equal to procrastination.

Have you ever said or heard someone else say that they never get the important things done. Or when I am under pressure I work better, they love to put tasks off to the last possible minute. Most peoples don't like the words have to do something. It like being forced to do something. Anytime you're being forced to do something you automatically feel a sense of resentment and rebellion. So what do you do? Well for starter the one thing I do know about life is that no-one have to do anything even though there are serious consequences, yet you are always free to choose.

There is other good news for instant even the worst procrastinators don't procrastinate all of the time. They never miss their favorite TV shows, or meet their friends at their favorite relaxing spot. You might even say that yes, I am a procrastinator and you still getting things done so you are not hurting anyone. Such thinking is dangerous. You must avoid the temptation to underestimate the seriousness of problems that on the surface may appear minor. Like most problems if they are not dealt with properly they will grow into a monster. Once you realize that the problem of procrastinating have been faced by millions of people. You have the will and the potential for dealing with this problem. Just remember that your reaction to the problem is as much of a problem as the problem itsel. And it will determine the outcome.

There will never be another now,

You must make the most of today.

There will never be another me,

I'll make the most of myself.

One sure way to beat old procrastination, just like NIKE commercial, "just do I t". but instead of doing the hold task at once. Break the task down in small pieces. Then start and finish one small piece at a time. To be successful at anything you much make up your mind to get going, one step at a time is all it takes.

SELF-IMAGE

Of all the obstacles and encouragements in an individual life, none is more significant than those that profoundly effect personal growth, developments and achievements. Your self-image better known as your inner mirror determined whether you live a life of impoverishment or prosperity. Everyone was born with a health free open self-image. Between birth and around nine or ten years old the mind absorbed enough data from its surrounding concerning: his looks, body parts, and others attributes to developed a non-publishable portrait of it self. This image was formed and is based upon someone else opinion of you and how they treated or mistreated you.

Unknown to most individuals someone else opinion is controlling how they think, feel, and act concerning themselves. A survey was conducted some years ago, and concluded that out of one hundred individuals, eighty-percent failed to live up to their full potential. Fifty-five percent of that eighty, will become complacent to live a life of mediocrity. The remaining twenty-five percents will forever depend on governmental assistant for their basic necessities of life.

WHAT IS SELF-IMAGE?

Self-Image is the way you see yourself through your own eyes and the value that YOU place on your own life. It can be either positive or negative. It has been said that Self-image is the cousin to self-esteem and self-confidence, but in reality it has more to do with the likes and dislikes of the individual staring back at his or herself through a mirror. Self-image is the foundation for self-esteem and self-confidence. All three are correlated and codependent on each other for their own survival from life's many challenges. When you stand in front of the mirror, how do you feel about the person staring back at you? No matter how you feel, you need to know that the physical aspect of self-image can be manipulated by expensive clothes, jewels, exercises, even surgeries. How you see yourself through your own eyes becomes a picture or image even if no mirror is present. This self contained image is more important than the image staring back from the mirror. However no amount of accessories or surgeries can repair a damaged self-image without getting therapeutic treatments first.

NEGATIVE SELF-IMAGE

A negative self-image is abnormal, unhealthy, and should be avoided at all causes. A negative self-image is a dysfunction of the mind that dislikes the portrait inside of the individual and not necessarily the picture image of him looking back from the mirror. The thing with an individual with a negative self-image for them is nothing they do is ever good enough. Their body is either too skinny, fat or something is wrong with their nose, mouth, eyes or other body parts. The image inside of himself at times question his own existing here on earth. No individual was born with this frame of thinking. Where did it come from? In most cases this mind set was perpetuated by friends and family members during childhood. In my own life, I remember being dropped off at different family members' houses. Each time I was treated as an outsider. I developed a bad stuttering problem because someone was always telling me to shut up, be quiet, or don't open your mouth anymore. I was afraid to speak, for the fear of getting my face slapped or facing embarrassment.

At the age five or six I got a real bad ear infection in my right ear, it ran continuously, sometimes without me knowing it. Someone would point to my ear and say something disgusting about me or my situation. Apparently no one in my immediate family though that I needed to go to the doctor, because of this I suffered some hearing lost in my right ear. Because of the way I was hearing sounds, I began to speak poorly. For the rest of my school life I was teased about this. My grandmother, who finally reared my older brother and I, was already in her seventies and couldn't read or write. Memory of my childhood life was filled with indifference. I didn't believe that another family anywhere was as poor as we were. We had no running water, soap, combs, or toothbrushes. There was an outhouse about two hundred yards from the house. During the summer months you could smell it from two or three miles down the road, depending on which way the wind blew.

One of the houses we lived in caught fire. Someone told my grandmother that, had she cut the electricity off that night she could have saved the house. For the next seven or eight years, when the sun went down she would cut the power off to the house, even during the summer months. Because of food spoilages, I quickly became a vegetarian. My grandmother taught us that boys shouldn't bathe but once a month and two pairs of pants was sufficient for the whole school year. We would use lard, fish grease, or some other cooking oil to grease our face, head and arms with. The wood burning stove and smoke that it produced made me smell like smoked meat many school days. My appearance was so bad that whenever the teacher called on me to take part in the lesson, I would shy away or read so fast that I left everyone with their mouths open wondering what just happened. I'm telling you this because I developed a real bad case of inferiority.

My self-image was so low that you could have bought me with a nickel and got change back. I couldn't understand why we lived in the greatest country in the world with opulent all around me, but we couldn't enjoy it. For years I didn't like my self, didn't know how to approach girls, and was afraid to raise my hand. Even if the answer to a question jumped into my mouth, I was afraid to speak it. Out of approximately two hundred and fifty students my brother and I graduated number two hundred forty-eight and two hundred forty-nine respectively. Number two hundred fifty dropped out two months earlier. My older brother passed away last year. He never experience the touch or the smell of a woman.

POSITIVE SELF-IMAGE

If you are fortunate enough to have a positive self-image then you have a leg up on life. Because of the self love you have already made, life awaits you with open arms. All you have to do is embrace it. A positive self-image is normal, healthy and greatly rewarding to the individual that possesses it. Obtaining it should be everyone's goal. The legendary speaker and electrifying motivator, Zig Ziglar, every now and then would play a game with his audiences just to show them the power of a positive self-image. So just for a moment let's play a little game. It's early in the morning and your telephone rings. You enthusiastically pick up the receiver like you always do. You say, good morning, it's a great day to be alive, how can I help you? The voice on the other end of the phone says hey pal its great that you're feeling so good, by the time I finish talking, you should feel even better. I intended to call you for a long time now, and I apologize for not calling you sooner. What I wanted to tell you is that I think that you are one the nicest persons I've ever met. You are a credit to your organization. You are an asset to your community. When I'm around you I am entreated, enthusiastic, and man I am motivated! If I could just spend fifteen minutes with you everyday, man I could turn this world up-side down!! No no I didn't call to borrow any money. I just wanted to let you know that I enjoy talking to you and I look forward to speaking with you again. With that the caller hands up the phone.

Now let me ask you a question, if you would ever receive a call like that or if you receive a call like that say in the next two or three days from now, how would that make you feel? Well let me ask you this—if you were baking a cake, couldn't you bake a better cake? In that case let me ask you this , how much more did you know about baking a cake after the phone call then you knew before the call? You didn't know anymore now did you? Still something happened, that caller said that you were a credit to your organization, an asset to your community, and you weren't about to question his fine opinion of you. That caller fed your ego there by lifting up your self-image. You can be that caller everyday of your life. You can call on him or her as often as you like to or whenever you like to.

DEVELOPING A POSITIVE SELF-IMAGE

Children in particular are vulnerable to accepting false negative judgment from authority figures, because they have yet to developed competency in evaluating such reports. Because of this negative evaluation from family members and friends, the children developed a negative self-image or self hate. The good news is that if you don't have a positive self-image, there are ways to developed one. But It want be easy. Because you have lived with this self-hate for so long, deep down inside, you really believe that you are no good and your self-worth is nothing compared to others. The first thing that you must do if you want to have a more positive image; you must resolve to stop trying to determine your self-worth and values by someone else evaluation of you or the mistake of your past. These three things will at least put you on the right road to a more positive self-image.

1. Take inventory of your compatibilities.
2. Become your own best friend.
3. Do not let your past define you.

CHANGE YOUR HABITS-CHANGE YOUR LIFE

It true if you would like to get an idea of where you will be one year from today; just look back at what you were doing a year ago. Life has a way of mirroring itself. We all have habits some are good and some are bad. We sometimes find ourselves falling short when things aren't going our way. The way to change your life for the best is to create good habits. But to be successful with these new habits, you need to take baby steps over an extended period of time. To maintain this momentum you must acquire self-discipline. Without discipline you're find your self slipping again. One good question to ask your self is what do you want to accomplish and why? In order to take the necessary action you need to find out what is driving you. This is your motivation. This is the your reason for getting out of bed in the morning. When you look at successful people you're find that they adopt certain behaviors that pushes them in the direction that they desire. You will spend many hours looking for things or sorting through things when you don't keep things neat, clean, and organized. This is one habit changes that would work better for all of us. Another great habit to have is to take action when you have a clear vision, understanding of what you wish to obtain. Considerable research has demonstrated that most successful people displays certain characteristics or disposition. They have patterns of thinking and behaving in intelligent ways and are displayed when confronted with the problems of everyday living. I know that some people may not like the word "slave", because nobody wants to be a slave to anything or anybody. Yet every day of our life we are bound by habits. From the types of foods that we eat, to the time that we go to bed and get up. Even the people we associate with from day to day are habits. Like I said early there are good habits and there are bad habits. You can really see your habits at work if you drink or smoke. You do them around the same time each day or night. My question to you is since you are going to be a slave anyway to habits; what kind of slave do you wish to be?

1. A slave to good habits or
2. A slave to bad habits.

A good friend of mine once said that certain periods in her life she's accomplished a lots more by just letting things slide. Actually the opposite is true. Suppose you just let your housework slide; you will find yourself working twice as hard trying to get things back in order. You know once you start doing something good or bad it become a habit and after a period of time it become second nature. So we all can agree that to become successful we need to form good habits. Why not tackler them as a New Year Resolution. Let's say that each month I will develop one new good habit. I have a habit that I will do twenty push-ups every day. Now I can't just say this without having some way of verification. I have a chart , this is my written verification. Before I go to bed I say my prayer and check my chart to be sure that I have completed my push-ups for that day. The next month I may add some set-ups or jumping jacks. You can do this with anything but you must have a way of checking and balancing yourself.

HABITS THAT'S KILLING US

Smoking and Drinking kill more people than all diseases combined

Started back around 1985, the major tobacco companies have to provide a annually report to the U.S. Department of Health and Human Services a list of all ingredients added to tobacco in the manufacture of cigarettes. Supposedly the Health and Human Services are required to notify the U.S. Congress of any concerns it may have with any ingredients on that list. These additives make cigarettes more acceptable to the consumer. They make cigarettes milder and easier to inhale, improve taste, prolong burning, and shelf life. To be fair to the tobacco companies, there are a few cigarette out there that contain no additives at all and some that only contain a small portion of these ingredients. So here is an **A to Z** list of those ingredients.

A
- » Acetanisole
- » Acetic Acid
- » Acetoin
- » Acetophenone
- » 2-Acetylpyrazine
- » 2-Acetypyridine
- » 3-Acetypyridine
- » 2-Acetythiazole
- » Aconitic Acid
- » Dl-Alanine(1-Alanine)

- » Alfalfa Extract
- » Allspice Oil
- » Allyl Hexanoate
- » Alpha-Methlbenzy acetate
- » Ambergris Tincture
- » Ammonium Alginate
- » Ammonium Hydroxide
- » Ammonium Phosphate Dibasic
- » Amyl Alcohol
- » Amyl Butyrate
- » Amyl Formate
- » Amyl Octanoate
- » Alpha-Amylcinnamaldehyde
- » Amyris Oil, Trans-Anethole
- » Angelica Root (extract and oil)
- » Anisyl Acetate
- » Anisyl Alcohol
- » Anisyl Formate
- » Apple Juice Concentrate and extract
- » Apricot Extract
- » 1-Arginine
- » Ascorbic Acid
- » 1-Aspartic Acid

B
- » Balsam Peru and Oil
- » Bay Oil
- » Beeswax (resinoid and absolute)
- » Beet Juice Concentrate
- » Benzaldehyde
- » Benzaldehyde Glyceryl Acetal
- » Benzoic Acid
- » Benzoin (resin, resinoid, gum, and absolute)
- » Benzophenone benzyl Alcohol
- » Benzyl Benzoate
- » Benzyl Butyrate
- » Benzyl Cinnamate

» Benzyl Salicylate
» Bergamot Oil
» Bois De Rose ({eruvian) oOil bornyl Acetate
» Brown Sugar
» Buchu Leaf Oil
» 1-3-Butanediol
» 4-(2-butenylidene)-3
» Butyl Acetate
» Butyl Alcohol
» Butyl Butyrate
» Butyl Butyryl Lactate
» N-Butyl Isovalerate
» Butyl Phenylacetate
» 3-Butylidenephthalide
» Butyric Acid

C
» Camphene
» Cananga Oil
» Caramel and Caramel Color
» Caraway Oil
» Carbon
» Carbon Dioxide
» Cardamom Oleoresin (oil, extract, seed oil, and powder)
» Carob Bean and extract
» Beta-Carotene
» Carrot (oil and seed)
» Caarvacrol
» 4-Carvomenthenol
» 1-Carvone
» Beta-Caryophyllene Oxide beta-Caryophyllene
» Cascarilla Oil (and bark extract)
» Cassia (bark, buds, oil and extract) cassie Absolute
» Castoreum (extract t, tincture, liquid, and absolute)
» Cedar leaf Oil
» Cedarwood Oil Terpenes
» Celery Seed (extract, solid, oil, and oleoresin)

- » Cellulose (and Cellulose Fiber)
- » Chamomile Flower (oil and extract)
- » Chicory Extract
- » Chocolate
- » 1-8-Cineole
- » Cinnamaldehyde
- » Cinnamic Acid
- » Cinnamon Leaf (oil, bark oil, and extract)
- » Cinnamyl Acetate
- » Cinnamyl Alcohol
- » Cinnamyl Cinnamate
- » Cinnamyl Isovalerate
- » Citral
- » Citric Acid
- » Citronella Oil
- » Dl-Citronellol
- » Citronellyl Isobutyrate
- » Civet Absolute
- » Clary Sage Oil and Extract
- » Cocoa (cocoa shells, extract, distillate, powder, alkalized, absolute and tincture)
- » Coffee (and coffee solid extract)
- » Cognac (white and green oil)
- » Copaiba Oil
- » Coriander (extract, oil, and seed)
- » Corn Silk
- » Corn Syrup
- » Costus Root Oil
- » Para-Cymene
- » 1-Cysteine

D

- » Dandelion Root Solid Extract
- » Davana Oil
- » 2,4-Decadienal
- » Delta-Decalactone
- » Gamma-Decalactone

» Decanal
» Decanoic Acid
» Decanoic Acid
» Ester with 1,2,3—Propanetriol Octanoate (Coconut Oil)
» Dextrin
» Diacetyl
» Diethyl Malonate
» 2,3-Diethylpyrazine
» 5,7-Dihydro-2-<ethylthieno (3,4-d)
» Pyrimidine
» Dill Oil
» Meta-Dimethoxybenzene
» Para-Dime thoxybenzene
» 2,6-Dimethoxyphenol
» 3,4-Dihydrofuran-2-one
» 6,10-Dimethyl-1,3,6-Octatriene
» 4,5-Dimethyl-3-hydroxy-2,5-Dihydrofuran-2-one
» 6,10-.Dimethyl-5,9-undecadien-2-one
» 3,7-Dimethyl-6-octenoic acid, alpha, para-Dimethylbenzyl Alcohol
» Alpha, Alpha-Dimethylphenetyhyl butyrate
» 2,3-Dimethylpyrazine
» 2,5-Dimethylpyrazine
» 2,6-Dimethylpyrazine
» Delta-Dodecalactone
» Gamma-Dodecalactone

E
» Ethyl 2-Methylbutyrate
» Ethyl Acetate
» Ethyl Acetoacetate
» Ethyl Alcohol (including Specially Denatured Alcohol SDA No. 4)
» Ethyl Benzoate
» Ethyl Butyrate
» Ethyl Cinnamate
» Ethyl Decanoate

» Ethyl Heptanoate
» Ethyl Hexanoate
» Ethyl Isovalerate
» Ethyl Lactate
» Ethyl Laurate
» Ethyl Levulinate
» Ethyl Maltol
» Ethyl Methyl Phenylglycidate
» Ethyl Myristate
» Ethyl Nonanoate
» Ethyl Octadecanoate
» Ethyl Octanoate
» Ethyl Oleate
» Ethyl Palmitate
» Ethyl Phenylacetate
» Ethyl Propionate
» Ethyl Valerate
» Ethyl vanillin
» Ethyl Vanillin Glucoside
» 2-Ethyl-1-Hexanol
» 3-Ethyl-2-Hydroxy-2-Cyclopenten-1-One
» 2-Ethyl-3,(5 or 6)-Dimethylpyrazine
» 5-Ethyl-3-Hydroxy-4-Methyl-2(5H)-Furanone
» 2-Ethyl-3-Me thylpyrazine
» 4-Ethylbenzaldehyde
» 4-Ethylguaiacol,
» Para-Ethylguaiacol
» 3-Ethylpyridine

F

» **Farnesol**
» **Fenchone**
» **Fenugreek (extract, resin, and absolute)**
» **Fig Juice (concentrate and extract)**
» **Food Starch Modified**
» **Fructose**
» **Furfuryl Mercaptan**

» 4-(2-Furyl)-3-buten-2-one

G
» Galbanum (oil and resinoid)
» Geraniol
» Geranium Rose and Bourbon Oil
» Geranyl Acetate
» Geranyl Butyrate
» Geranyl Formate
» Ginger Oil and Oleoresin
» Glucose/Dextrose
» 1-Glutamic Acid
» Glycerol
» Graphite
» Guaiac Wood Oil
» Guaiacol
» Guar Gum

H
» 2,4-Heptadienal Gamma
» Heptalactone
» Heptanoic Acid
» 2-He[tanone
» #-Hepten-2-one3
» 4-Heptenal
» Heptyl acetate omega-6
» Hhexadecenlactone gamma
» Hexalactone
» Hexanal Hexanoic acid
» 2-Hexen-1ol
» 3-Hexen-1-ol cis-3
» Hexen-1-yl acetate
» Hexen-2-al
» 3_hexenoic acid trans-2
» Hexenoic acid cis-3
» Hexenyl formate protein

» 4-Hydroxybutsnoiv svif lsvyonr
» Hyftocyviytoellal
» 6-Hyfroxydihydrotheaspirane
» 4-(para-Hydroxyphenyl)-2-butanone
» Hydroxypropyl cellulose

I

» Immortelle (absolute and extract)
» Invert sugar
» Alpha-Ionone
» Beta-Ionone
» Isoamyl Acetate
» Isoamyl Benzoate
» Isoamyl Butyrate
» Isoamyl Cinnamate
» Isoamyl Formate
» Isoamyul Hexanoate
» Isoamyl Isovalerate
» Isoamyl Phenylacetate
» Isobutyl Acetate
» Isobuty Alcohol
» Isobuty Cinnamate
» Isobutyl Phenylacetate
» 2-Isobutyl-3-Methoxypyrazine
» Alpha-Isobutylphenethyl Alcohol
» Isobuy tyraldehyde
» Isobutyric Acid
» 2-Isopropylphenol
» Isovaleric acid

J

» Jasmine (absolute)

K

» Kola nut extract

L

»   Labdanum (oils, absolute)
»   Lactic Acid
»   Lauric Acid
»   Lavandin Oil
»   Lemon Oil
»   Lemongrass Oil
»   Levulinic Acid
»   Licorice (root, fluid extract and powder)
»   Lime Oil terpeneless)
»   Linalool
»   Linalool Oxide
»   Linalyl Acetate
»   L-:usine
»   Lovage Oil (and extract)

M

»   Mace (powder and oil)
»   1_Malic Acid
»   Malt (and malt extract)
»   Maltodextrin
»   Maltol
»   Mandarin (and tangerine oil)
»   Maple Syrup
»   Mate (leaf, absolute, extract and oil)
»   Para-Mentha-8-thiol-3-one
»   Menthol and L-Menthol
»   Menthone
»   Menthyl Acetate
»   Menthyl Isovalerate 2-5
»   6-Methoxy-4-vinylphenol,
»   Para-Methoxybenzaldehyde
»   1-(para-Methoxyphenyl)-1-penten-3-one

» 1_(para-Methoxyphenyl)-2-propanone
» Methoxypyrazine
» Methyl 2-furoate
» Methyl 2-octynoate
» Methyl 2-pyrrolyl ketone
» Para-Mthyl anisate
» Methyl anthranilate
» Methyl benzoate
» Methyl cinnamate
» Methyl dihydrojasmonate
» Methyl ester of rosin (partially hydrogenated)
» Methyl Isovalerate
» Methyl linoleate (48%)
» Methyl linolenate (52%) mixture
» Methyl phenylacetate
» Methyl salicylate
» Methyl sulfide
» 5-Methyl-2-phenyl-2-hexenal
» 6-Methyl-3,5-heptadien-2-one
» 1-Methyl-3-methoxy-4-isopropyibenzene
» Methyl-3-methylthiopropionate
» 2-Methyl-4-phenylbutyraldehyde
» 6-Methyl-5-hepten-2-one
» 4-Methyl-5-thiazoleethanol
» 4-Methylacetophenone
» Methyl-alpha-ionone
» Para-Methyicinnamaldehyde
» Methylcyclopentenolone
» 2-Methylheptanoic Acid
» 2-Methylhexanoic Acid
» 3-Methylpentanoic Acid
» (Methylthio) methylpyazine (mixture of isomers)
» 2-Methylpyrazine
» 5-Meth7yquinoxaline
» 3-(methyulthio) propionaldehyde
» Methyl-tran-2-butenoic acid
» 2-Methylvaleric acid
» Mimosa absolute

- » Molasses (blackstrap, sugarcane and extract)
- » Mountain maple solid extract
- » Myristic acid
- » Myrrh (oil and absolute)

N

- » Nerol
- » Neroli bigarade oil
- » Nerolidol
- » Nona-2-trans, 6-cis-dienal
- » 2,6-Nonadien-1-ol,gammma
- » Nonalactone
- » Nonanal
- » Nonanoic acid
- » 2-Nonanone, trans-2-nonen-1-ol
- » Nonyl alcohol
- » Nutmeg (powder and oil)

O

- » Oak moss absolute
- » 9,12-Octadecadienoic acid (48%) and 9,12,15-octadecatrienoic acid (52%)(mixture)
- » Delta-Octalactone gamma-Octalactone
- » Octanal
- » Octanoic acid
- » 2-Octanone
- » 1-Octen-3-ol
- » 2-trans-Octenal
- » Octyl Isobutyrate
- » Oleic acid
- » Olibanum Oil
- » Opoponax Oil

» Oarange l eaf absolute
» Orange Oil (sweet orange oils terpeneless, sour/bitter orange oils)
» Orange oil and extract (sweeet, distilled orange oils and terpenless)
» Origanum Oil
» Orris concrete (oil and root extract)

P

» Palmarosa oil
» Palmitic acid
» Parsley seed oil
» Patchouly oil and absolute
» Pectin
» Omega-Pentadecalactone
» 2,3-Pentanedione
» 2-Pentanone
» Pepper oil
» Black Peppermint (oil and peppermint oil terpeneless)
» Petitgrain (absolute, oil and terpeneless oil)
» Alpha-Phellandrene
» 2-Phenethyl Acetate
» Phenethyl Alcohol
» Phenethyl Phenylacetate
» 3-Phenyl-1-Peopanol
» 2-Phenyl-2-butenal
» 4-Phenyl-3-buten-2-one
» Phenylacetaldehyde
» Phenylacetic acid
» 1-Phenylalanine
» 3-Phenylpropionaldehyde
» 3-Phenylpropionic acid
» 3-Phenylpropyl acetate
» Phosphoric acid
» Pine needle oil

» Pine oil, scotch
» Pineapple Juice concentrate
» Alpha-Pinene
» Beta-Pinene
» Piperonal
» Pipsissewa leaf extract
» Plum Juice concentrate and extract
» Potassium Carbonate
» Potassium sorbate
» 1-Proline
» Paropenylguaethol
» Propionic acid
» Propyl acetate
» Propyl para-Hydroxbenzoate
» Propylene Glycol
» 3-Propylidenephthalide
» Prune Juice and concentrate
» Pyridine
» Pyroligneous acid and extract
» Pyruvic acid

R

» Raisin Juice (concentrate and extract)
» 1-Rhamnose
» Rhodinol rose (absolute and oil)
» Rosemary (oil and extract) rum (and rum extract
» Rum ether
» Rye Extract

S

» Sage (oil, oleoresin, and powder)
» Salicylaldehyde
» Sandalwood (oil, yellow)

- » Sclareolide
- » Sodium benzoate
- » Sodium Bicarbonate
- » Sodium carbonate
- » Sodium Citrate
- » Sorbic Acid
- » D-Sorbitol
- » Spearmint Oil
- » Storax (and styrax, extract, gum and oil)
- » Sucrose
- » Sucrose Octaacetate

T

- » Tagetes oil
- » 1_Tartaric acid
- » Dl_Tartaric acid tea extract
- » Alpha-Terpineol
- » Terpinolene
- » Alpha-Terpinyl acetate
- » 5,6,7,8-Tetrahydroquinoxaline
- » 1,5,5,9-Tetramethyl-13-oxatricyclo (8.3.0.0(4,9)
- » Tridecane,2,3,5,6-Tetramethylpyrazine
- » Thyme oil
- » Thymol
- » Tolu balsam gum, resinoid, and extract tolualdehydes (ortho,meta,para)
- » Para-Tolyl3-methylbutyrate
- » Para-Tolyl acetate
- » Para-Tolyl isobutyrate
- » Para-Tolyl phenylacetate
- » Triacetin
- » 2-Tridecanone
- » Triethyl citrate
- » 3,5,5-Trimethyl-1-1hexanol
- » 4-(2,6,6-Trimethylcyclohex-1-enyl)but-2-en-4-one
- » 2,6,6-Trimethylcyclohex-2-ene-1,4-dione
- » 4-(2,6,6-Trimethylcyclohexa-1,3-dienyl)but-2-en-4-one
- » 2,6,6-Trimethylcyclohexanone

» **2,3,5-Trimethylpyrazine**

U

» Delta-Undecalactone
» Gamma-Undecalactone
» 2-Undecanone
» Urea

V

» **Valeraldehyde**
» **Valerian root (extract, oil and owder)**
» **Valeric acid**
» **Gamma-Valerolactone**
» **1-Valine vanilla extract and oleresin**
» **Vanillin**
» **Veratraldehyde**
» **Vetiver oil**
» **Violet leaf absolute**
» **Vanilla extract and oleresin**
» **Vanillin**
» **Veratraldehyde**
» **Vetiver oil**
» **Violet leaf absolute**

W

» **Walnut hull extract**
» **Water**
» **Wheat absolute**
» **Wine and wine sherry**

Y

» **Ylang ylang oil**

YOU DON'T HAVE TO SMOKE

With all of these additives that possible could be in cigarette, some good, some bad. You don't have to smoke, so why take unnecessary chances with your life? We all have heard the warning that cigarettes can cause cancer and increase the risk of heart disease and others health problems. Do you know that smoking is the most preventable cause of death in the world? Oh yes! Smoking, is the number one cause of preventable death in the United States too. Smoking kill more Americans than alcohol, AIDS, car accidents, illegal drugs, suicides and murders combined. Approximately 200.000 Americans will be diagnosed with lung cancer this year; eighty percent of those cases will be caused by smoking. What ever your goal in life is..whatever it is that you are trying to achieve, isn't worthy the paper its written on if you'll not around to enjoy it.

Smoking is detrimental to your health, your family, your friends and your neighbors. Smoking is a bad habit, it binds it's victims. Everyone should take a stand against smoking, because we all must breath air to live. In poor ventilated rooms, when one person smoke, we all do. Smoking defiles the body which is God's temple. Cigarette cost about five or more dollars per pack, which make it an expensive habit as well. We need to get into God's words daily so we can built up our strength. Take a few minutes out your busy scheduler and think on these verses.

1. **Ye are bought with a price: Therefore glorify God in your body, and in your spirit, which are God's. 1 Corinthians 6:20**
2. **Know ye not that ye are the temple of God: and that the spirit of God dwelleth in you? If any man defile the temple of God,**

him shall God destroy. For the temple of God is holy. Which temple ye are? 1Corinthians 3:16-17

SOME OTHERS REASONS TO QUIT SMOKING

» You'll be less wrinkly, smoking can speed up your skin's aging process by narrowing your skin's blood vessels and damaging the tissues that give the skin its strength and elasticity.

» Stop or cutting back on smoking , will save you money.

» Nonsmokers have stronger bones than smokers.

» Stop smoking might fix that ringing sound that most smokers hear in their ears. Not to mentioned that nagging cough.

» May not get Psoriasis. Some studies shows that daily smoking is linked to the risk of developing Psoriasis.

» Cut back on certain medication, when you cut back on smoking.

» If you stop smoking, you'll less likely to burn down your house.

» Smoking increases the risk of Dementia.

» Studies shows that cigarette smoking harms some women ovaries.

» When you stop smoking, you stop being a bad influence on children/

» Preserve your eyesight from Muscular Degeneration.

» Cut down on the amount of poisons that goes into your body ever time you light one up. Cigarette smoke contains some 4000 chemical agents, about 3990 of them you can not name or spell.

» When you cut down on smoking, you also cut down on the amount of your life insurance too.

» Delay the onset of Menopause's.

» Avoid carbon monoxide and other well known killer.

» Your breath will be fresher.

» You'll enjoy your food more—quitting smoking will bring back your sense of taste.

» Stop smoking will preserve your sense of smell. If a smoker could smell their breath, their car, their clothes and their hair, they're probably quit sooner.

ALCOHOL NOT JUST A HABIT IT'S ALSO A KILLER

Alcohol has the ability to alter people pattern of attitude, and behavior. This is one of the main reason why a person who consume alcohol may do things or act in a way that he or she wouldn't normally do. Statistics shows that 15,000 people died as a result of their drinking. Most people do not realize how many of the body's systems are affected by alcohol and the relationship between alchol and cancer, particularly cancer of the digestive system and possible breast cancer as well.

BENEFITS OF DRINKING ALCOHOL

According to the National Institute on alcohol abuse and alcoholism, it concluded, after much scientific reviews that moderate drinkers, do have lower death rate compare to heavy drinkers and some who don't drink. Scientific finding that moderate drinkers do have stable heart condition, therefore improve their longevity.

ALCOHOL POISONING

Approximately 50, 000 cases of alcohol poisoning are reported each year in the United States. Alcohol poisoning is when someone consume too much alcohol. The poisoning come into play when an individual drink more than his or hher body can metabolize. And yes you can die from ingesting too much alcohol. In fact someone needlessly dies from alcohol poisoning every week.

FACTORS THAT AFFECT YOUR BLOOD ALCOHOL LEVEL

When you drank, there are factors that influenced the effect the alcohol will have on your body; and they are:

1. **How much alcohol you consumed**
2. **How quickly your body metabolizes the alcoholism**
3. **How strong the alcoholic drink**
4. **How quickly you consume the alcohol drink**

5. Your body weight.

SIGNS AND SYMPTON OF ALCOHOL POISONING

» **Absent Reflexes**
» **Erratic Behavior**
» **Seizure**
» **No feeling from painful stimulation**
» **Slurred Speech**
» **Unconsciousness**
» **Inability to make eye contact or sustain a conversation**
» **Feeling very ill – vomiting**
» **Slow, shallow, irregular breathing**

DRINKING TOO MUCH

Back in the days when I was much younger, I thought that drinking alcohols would make be look and feel cool. From the time I tasted that God forsaken juice on my tongue and felt that sensational sparking rushed to my head; I was hooked. Because of my low self esteem and inferiority complexion. I found a friend that made me feel as good if not better then any human being could. The truth is I needed a drink to help me come out of my shell. Many times I hit rock bottom although I didn't want to admit it but getting into fights, being slopped, falling down drunk and losing a job or two, told a difference story. I was a victim to alcohol and it pervaded every area of my life. My friends and I would drink, drink and drink ourselves drunk and broke at the same times. But I never considered my self being an alcoholic. Now that I am older and looking back, I can honesty say that I made some bad decisions. That why I know down to my very being, that God is good all the times. Some of the situation I have been evolved in, without God watching over me I would not be writing this book right now.

THE NEGATIVE EFFECTS OF DRINKING TOO MUCH

No matter what you do in life; please remember this, to include eating and anything else. Even drinking water, do it in moderation. Things that's suppose to be good for you, if you abuse or misuse them can quickly become bad for you. Some people never touch the stuff until they get depressed. The one thing that I can tell you for sure is that drinking while you are depressed will only make you feel more depressed. When you drink too much alcohol there will be some short term as well as long time effect. Anything that causes you to lose coordination, blind vision, slurring of speech, lost of balance and a lack of judgment can't be good for you. In the last chapter we talked about smoking being a bad habit, well lady and gentlemen drinking too much is a bad habit too. In fact if you drink too much you can experience extreme negative effect. For example; unconsciousness, coma and unlike smoking you can die the same day. I never heard of anybody smoking themselves to death in the same day or same night. Seriously, folks alcoholism is a very serious problem that should not be taking lightly.

DO MORE, GIVE MORE THAN WHAT'S EXPECTED

In order to enjoy the fruits of enduring success, man must be willing to do more than what is expected of him. This important principle is taught in every regions of the world. It has held truth in the beginning of time and hold true today. In all walk of life and every job situation as well, most people love to get a little bit more than what they paid for. Someone having the reputation of doing just a bit more than what was required to get a job done will more than likely get a promotion or make more money than someone who do or give just the minimal. We live in a world or mediocrity. We meet people on a daily basis who seen as if they woke up on the wrong side of the bed. Isn't it refreshing when we meet someone who is courteous or go beyond their job description to help you? These are people who make an everlasting impression upon your life as well as their own. The other person make an everlasting impression also, but it will be remember in a negative way. Going the extra mile benefit everybody concern. You know nature applies this line of thinking very well. Take farming or just your everyday gardener for instant; for all of the hard work that must be done before the seed even touched the ground. The land must be cleared, plowed and even the seeds must be planted at the right time, for opulent production they must be exactly spaced. Then and only after the farmer or gardener done their duty, nature step in and for all of their hard work mind you , the work that he have not been compensated for yet, the seeds is germinated and reproduction take place, through the law of increasing returns or values returns each seed yields him perhaps a hundred time over. No one can make or compelled you to do more or give more than what's required of you. But if you do, compensation may not come in the form of your expectations, never-the-less, they will come. Some benefits or compensations are:

1. You're develops a positive mental attitude.
2. Job security.
3. Stimulate your soul.
4. Increase pay.
5. Promotion.
6. Better relationship.
7. Clear conscience.
8. Build character.

Doing more than is expected also mean to give more than is expected. Imagine the meat department in a grocery store that gives an extra piece of meat to his customers. Those customers not only will return, they will also recommend their friends, family members and others to do business with him. It hard to lose when you follow nature rules, and yet some business owner gives you just the right amount, sometimes even less. I say this over and over again if you follow the rules, of giving more or doing more you cannot go wrong. But let's us be frank; not everyone that you encounter is going to appreciate you no matter what you give or do for them, this is a fact of life. Accept this fact and continues to do what you do-that is to do more and give more. Because one day, the reward could far exceed everything, every mile you ever walked for all your customers, family or friends combined. In the military I learn that going above and beyond the call of duty was one true way to add significant, lasting, and memorable value to my squad, team, platoon or company.

ATTITUDE

"Attitude is everything". But I want to convey to you that not only is attitude everything, but a positive attitude is one of the keys to success. Without a positive attitude the only things you will attract in your life is negativity. Some of us wake up in the morning with a frown on our face. Not even thankful for being able to wake up. We can't say hello or give the greeting of day to strangers. Now some of these are the same folks you see every Sunday at church, praising God. I don't go to church like I should but I was raise up in the church. I was taught that I was the church, so I carry God in my heart everywhere I go. Somewhere I remember reading a passive that ask the question, how can you say that you love God whom you have not seen, Yet you hate your brother whom you see every day? Many of you don't have anything good to say about anybody. It is impossible for a negative mind to attract positive things.

What's the old saying? If you go looking for trouble, nine times out of ten you will find it. The human brain is a master piece in itself. The man or woman who can control just ten percent of their mind will be worth millions if not billions of dollars. You see we have a conscious and a subconscious mind that most of the times do not see eye to eye. The conscious mind is always trying to make sense, trying to reason or used logic to come to a sounded decision. The subconscious mind is so great that it control ninety-nine percent of all body functions. Yet it cannot distinguish between negative and positive thoughts. So what ever you tell yourself over and over, eventually the subconscious will believe it. This is another key to success, that we will talk more about in a later chapter.

A doctor named Franschio, was trying to reprogram a pessimistic thinker. He first started by sending one positive thought to the person subconscious mind. But there were so many negative thoughts in the person mind that when ever he open the door and pushed that one positive thought in, it was quickly over-powered and killed by thousand of negative thoughts. After trying for many hours and days, the good doctor decided to let some of the negative thoughts come out and replace each negative thought that came out with five positive one. Soon there was enough positive thoughts to over-powered the negative one. But even when there was more positive thoughts then negative thoughts, the battle was in no way easy. It was a matter of conditioning; just as you have to continually train your body to stay in shape, the same is true with your mind. Just as you watch what foods you consume for optimum health the same is true for your mental health. From every phase of your life attitude plays a major part with the day to day function of life. Maintaining a positive mental attitude isn't easy.

Having a positive mental attitude is no way a guaranteed for success. But having a negative attitude is certain a recipe for failure. In life we have choices no matter what the situation may be. We can determine how a certain problem going to effect us mentally or physically. Always remember that anything that effect you mental will also effect you physically. But we can see our problems as an elephant or an opportunity. An old saying you may have heard; you may not have had anything to do with life knocking you down but you have everything to do with staying down. When I talk about attitude I am talking about stepping out of your body for a minute and looking back down at yourself lying or standing there. I know that you're saying that I have flipped my top. But I am serious, you must get away from looking at your problem the way you have always preceded them. That is most of your problem.

You got to change your level of thinking. The way that you look at your problems and your attitude concerning your problems changed your problems. we are our own worst enemy when it come to solving our problems. We cannot solve out problems with the same level of thinking that was there when we created the problem. In each one of us we bring to the table of problem solving our own emotions, ideals and family values. Before you ever began the task of solving the problem you come to the table prejudice. If you were in court, the judge would dismiss you from your own problem solving case. Many times we want other people to change, because we feel that they are the problem, your character and motives are the driving forces behind your problem solving. By being true to yourself, your attitude toward others will automatically take a turn inward.

The question was who among you without sin, cast the first stone. A marriage can be a beautiful or nasty thing. A match made in heaven or hell. The man or woman who doesn't have a sense of their own identity or self-worth will always have a conflicting marriage. Sometimes we could be moving too slow or too fast for our spouse. At times we empowering them and at times we may be over powering them or they could be overpowering us. The biggest obstacle to solving the problem lies in our attitude toward the problem.

SUCCESS

WHAT IS SUCCESS? Success is one of those peculiar words, because it means so much, or so little. To varied peoples. But I will tell you this, that success can be both positive and negative. Let me explain; success in itself is the end result of some action taking early. The outcome or types of success depend on what actions you took or didn't take. I'm talking about positive action that brings positive success and negative actions that bring about negative success. What I am trying to get across to you is whether you take action or not it will still bring about something. Suppose you are to be at work say 8 A. M. And the commute from your house to work take approximately twenty minutes; what happen if you decided to sleep until 7:45? you're more likely going to be late for work, which mean that lot's of things could result from your negative action of not getting out of bed early. You could be written up, could have an accident by rushing; maybe lose your job, or life.

On the other hand say you made it a habit of getting up and arriving to work fifteen minutes early each morning, this action could bring about a promotion, letter of commendation or a raise. This is positive action that brought about positive success. While I am on the conversation of actions, positive and negative, I have to reflex back on my own life. I grew up poor , you may say dirt poor. I graduate at the bottom of my class of about 250 students. I was one of the students voted less likely to become successful. I joined the army at seventeen with a bad inferiority complexion. This is the same time I started drinking, my military record is long with alcoholic related incidents. I have over twenty years of military services which mean I could have reach the top position in my profession. But instead I have to settle for being about average. Because my drinking wouldn't allow me to really apply myself like I needed to do to get the promotion and the positive recognition I needed to get ahead.

The drinking was just a by-product of me trying to hide my low self-esteem, trying to fit in with others that I thought was my friends. I had a bad habit of drinking, because it gave me courage. Often times that was too much courage going in the wrong direction, like fighting and being rebellion. Most of us have some type of habit that's keeping us from being a better man or woman. Some of these habits could ruin our lives for good. You would think if a man or woman awaken the next morning hung over, couldn't remember what happen the night before that it would be enough to make them want to quite all together. We drink or take other drugs for many reason. Millions of dollars in sales are made through these bad habits. In fact the people who have those habits will spend their last dime to keep those habits up. Some will supp;y their habits before they will buy food.

I have a brother who lived in Chicago, he just had a stroke. While talking to him he told me that he couldn't wait to get out of the hospital so that he could get his favorite drugs; rocks cocain, the same drug that caused him to have the stroke. He just said that it meant that the cocain was some good stuff, if it caused him to have a stroke, and he needed to catch that same guy who sold it to him before it was all gone. One thing drinking taught me, until a man or woman learn to have control over themselves, nothing else in this world really matter. I told you early that your actions will bring about some type of success. Positive success can be described as the aggressive realization of a worthy ideal. Simply put, success is doing what you like to do. Whether it being a stay at home mom or a janitor. If this what's makes you happy and this is what you want to do then you are successful.

This reminds me of a story I once heard. A man went to Africa and captured a parrot, turns him into a pet and taught him how to talk. The man fed the bird really well and gave him just about anything he wanted except letting him go free. One day some year later the man was talking to the bird concerning his upcoming trip back to Africa. The man asks the bird if he wanted to relate any information concerning him back to his friends and family. The bird told him to tell his family and friends that he was doing very well. He couldn't have found a better master nowhere. The man thanked the bird for his complement and off he went to Africa. Once in Africa the man met with the many family and friends of the parrot. He told them that the parrot said for them not to worry about him because he was doing very well and that he couldn't ask for a better home. While the man was still talking one of the parrot there started to cry and fell over dead. The man said to himself that the dead bird must have been a real close family member or a real good friend and just was overcome by the good news. Once the man returned back home he told the parrot what had taking place in Africa about the parrot dying. While the parrot in the cage listens to him he began to cry and started to shake and fell over dead.

The man was stunned, he thought to himself he should have kept that bad news to himself, if he had, his bird wouldn't be dead. The man went and got a shovel to dig a nice grave for his little friend. Once the grave was dug, the man with tear in his eyes, open the parrot cage and with care pick up his friend and laid him down beside the grave, while he ran back inside the house to get his bible. When he return he noted that the parrot was going. High above the man on a tree branch, the parrot told the man no words of pity for me today. For today and the rest of my life I will be free. The man asked the bird, why did he faked his death? The bird told him that this was the message that his friend sent him when the man came back from Africa and gave him the bad new of his friend dying.

The hidden message that the other bird sent him was that if you want to be free of your old situation, then you must die and be born again. How dare you to cage me up and just because you feed me well expect me to be happy that you came alone. Just like the bird did, to begin this journey of becoming successful you first must let yourself out of the cage, untie the rope or what ever the thing is that 's holding the positive you back.

Look in the mirror, ask a family member or ask a friend if you don't know the habit or habits that holding you down. In order to change you must become self discipline. I love the military definition of discipline: it is the individual or group attitude that ensure prompt obedience to order and the initiation of the approximately action in the absent of orders. You see to be discipline, you don't need someone standing over you with a stick or whip in order for you to do what is right. If someone is not looking at us , at all times we have a tendencies to get relaxed and complacence.

This is not self-discipline. Did you note that the definition started with the word attitude? I teach my children that attitude is everything. Your attitude in life should be that I am going to do what's right just because it is the right thing to do, period. You must become a master of self before you can master anything else on this earth. Become the captain of your own ship, then and only then can you sail anyway or anywhere you like.

DRESS FOR SUCCESS

By now, if you are still reading this, then I must have written something that got your attention. That's good because we are about to get into the bread and butter of this book. When I talk about dress for success, it is a profound thought. Whether you believe me or not, but the way you look speak volumes about you. I must tell you this. When I was a young boy I hated going to school. Not that I hated to learn or the teachers, but because of how I was dressed. With two pair of pants and a hand full of shirts to my name each school season, was terrifying. My peers would make bets on which pant or shirt I was going to wear for the next day.

The first week of the new school year was my best days of the whole school season. Because the two pairs of pants I had were new and clean, they made me feel good about myself. Unfortunately this only last about two weeks, by then my two pairs of pants had been seen five times each. I became a joke in school. I'm telling you this because the way I dressed had a direct reflection on my self-esteem, self-confident and motivation. I wasn't dressing like a winner and I didn't feel like one either.

When you look in the mirror what do you see? The you that you see is the you that you will be. How important do you feel? I have heard some individual say that they dress according to how they feel. Let me ask you this, if you wake up in the morning really in a bad mood; if you dress to this standard, you will be miserable for the rest of the day. Fresh, neat and clean clothes have a way of lifting your spirit. Before two people get near enough to speak, their attires have already spoken volumes about them.

The way you dress, I could possible tell something about your personality, mood and taste. Fair or not but people do judge or make decision about you based on your appearance. When I talk about dress for success I'm speaking in turn of your profession, business or what ever you want to convey to others about you. To be effective you much be competent in your own mind. So be very careful because clothes cover about 95% of our body and just as you are what you eat; you guess it! You are what you wear. Think about what you want to say with your appearance. If your profession is pluming you would look out of place arriving at a customer house with your toolbox wearing a suit. Remember this about the subject of dressing for success even if you don't remember nothing else, "first impression is forever".

CHOOSE TO BE SUCCESSFUL IT IS A CHOICE

According to Winston Churchill, "victory comes only to those who work hard and long who are willing to pay the price in; blood, sweat and tears."

No matter how difficult life become, the good news is that we have choices. Sometimes we don't feel like we have choices concerning out lives, but we do. Even when things go wrong as they sometimes will. Like getting behind on your gas or light bills or maybe losing your job. In these difficult moments you can choose to do something or you can choose to do nothing.either you choose your plan of action or life will force you to except it plan of action. At times in life you will be backed into a corner. The choice of how you come out of that corner is your and your along. At time the way you can come out of that corner are all bad choices. Still you get to make a choice between the two or more evils hoping that you choose the best one. The only way to win in life is to give yourself the option of choices so it will be hard at first because now you must change your way of thinking. But once you start the wheels turning there will be no stopping you. Yes you will be in control, it your life why not? Even if you fail, you are responsible; if you are successful, you are still responsible. No matter what life throw your way you have a choice as to how you are going to allow it to affect you.

Take marriages for instant, many ends in divorce. For one, most of us expect instant gratification when it doesn't come soon enough or I t seen to be too much work involved we want out in turn of divorce. Or we are expecting more from our husband and or wife than we're willing to give. It strange but true, but even to have a happy marriage simple put, it is a matter of choices. Life consist of many choices, a number of choices we make create anxiety disagreement while other choices make our lives more happier. Your success in life are directly related to the decisions that we make daily, some of us try to blame God for our failure because we feel that he allowed us to make a bad choice. But God don;t stop us from making the wrong decisions just liked he don't stop us from making the right decision. God has set in motion spiritual laws for us human that bring about good or bad result, depending on the choices we make. Obey God's laws and good results automatically happen. Break God's laws and bad results happen. Because of our selfish nature our flesh is weak.

Once we rise above our selfishness, we began to get stronger because now we are building God character. If we fail to understand this, then we fail to understand a great deal about God plan and purpose for us. Everybody wants to be happy. But everybody doesn't understand that happiness possesses the strength of character to making good choices. Imagine for a moment that you are watching your television and there is a movie about your life and the main character is you. From your chair or bed you watch as your life unfold. You watch the failures as well as the successes of your life. You watch as different relationships mature and change. You watch the ceremonies of a fully life lived, to include romances, unions, deaths and graduation. As you watch your movie imagines that you discover that your life is good and a happy one. What would you attribute to the success fulness of your life would you walk away from your movie and say "life dealt me a pretty good hand", or would you observe and reflect on certain events and say that I'm glad that I chose well?

SUCCESS IN THE FAMILY

What I am about to tell you will undoubtedly make many of you angry. My saying this does in no mean make me a saint or liar for that matter. I will be the first to say that I'm no priest or marriage counselor. But doing my forty some year on God blessed earth I have learn a few things. Way back a long time ago in the so called traditional marriage it seen that couple's stayed marriage for many more years than they do now. More and more couples were getting marriage and if they didn't the whole community would frown on them. These days we hear daily talks about same sex marriages. The traditional marriage appeal to be long gone and so too are family values. To have a lasting marriage for one you much be of equal yoke. The two o f you must have a number of things in common. You must have God in your life if your marriage is going to work. One thing you can say about Satan is that he loves turmoil, confusing and plain old mess. Without God in your life it like building a house without a good foundation, you won't have nothing but problem after problems. God is a solid foundation; for a marriage or anything else you have going on in your life. Not having God in their life is the main reason why half of all the couple marriage today will end in divorce.

GOOD COMMUNICATION: I'll found that couples who know how to talk to each others have a greater survivor rate then those who do not have good communication skills. Communication in marriage can be verbal or nonverbal. What you don't say is just as important as what you do say. Silence or withdraw hurt. It put a selfish image to work. Both couples trying to wait the other out. Neither want to be the first to give in. The longer the silence or withdraw goes on the better the chance for a ugly confrontation to take place. Both partners are playing the blame game inside of their own head. Even if non—verbal, communications still take place, the nonverbal signal that the two of you send out is enough to keep the confrontation going. Like not saying good night to each other when you go to bed. Sleeping in different bed, not cooking or cleaning up the house, don't tell the other good-night, good-bye or see you later. I'm not giving him or her any more money or just stop doing the things that you used to do are all nonverbal communication signifying that you are still angry, upset over some issues or others.

Dealing with conflict: no matter how great your marriage is; if it never had been tested then you won't know how strong it is. In marriage conflict is inevitable. But how you deal with it is a matter of choice. In some marriage the partners stop fighting about the real problem and began to fight each others. In a marriage you must agree to disagree and this must be done without trying to validate the problem by fault finding or hurling insults at each others.

BE COMMITTED TO THE MARRIAGE: I strongly believe that those couples who are committed to enchanting their marriage and making it work no matter what; will outlast many who at the first sign of trouble run for the hills. Not many people knew the first time they got marriage how to make it work, but are willing to do what ever it take for as long as it take to make it work will go a long ways in preserving their marriages. Marriage requires each couple to be equally committed to their own personal growths as well as their spouse. Marriage is something that you grow into each day. Each day is a n an important event in your marriage and you must work diligently on it. The first time you stop talking or start taking your marriage for granted, Satan will be right there to compound your problem with temptations and other amenities. Your marriage is Holy it had been sanctify by God, so automatically this makes Satan angry. Not only that, but he knows that when you have a great marriage your family is strong. In order for him to overthrow you—you have to let him in the front door keep on fighting about every little thing in your marriage that isn't perfect. Keep on with the name calling. Keep on putting your partner down. All of these are sure fire ways to allow Satan excess into your marriage. Just remember Satan don't just want to break you all up. No sir! He want stop there, what he's really after is something that you don't feel a need of right now and don't know just how important it is, that is your soul. In a sense this had nothing to do with you physically but everything to do with you spiritually. It is an on going battle between good and evil and by taking your soul it is a personal attack on God himself.

KNOW YOUR ROLE IN THE MARRIAGE: In previous traditional marriages, each partner knew their role. Because of equal right for women now, both sexes are equally able to perform nearly all of the tasks required in a marriages. Neither has to depend on the other. What's used to be men work have fast become women work and vice verse. You can't even ask the question of who wear the pant or boots in the house with any meaning because both male and female wear the same. Isn't it funny that soon after a beautiful wedding and all of the firework have fiddler out that what started out with good intention now hand together by a shoestring? You must understand the role that love lays in the family , in order to have a successful marriage. I will talk to you more on the subject of love in the another chapter.

FAILURE IS NOT AN OPTION

The dictionaries define failure as: a weakening, a breakdown in operation, neglect, not succeeding, a failure to pass. I believe that failure is the inability to get up when you fall down. Now as I always say; you may not have anything to do with being knocked down but you have everything to do with staying down. In-fact some of the most successful people in the world got their status in life through many failures time and time again. There is always a lesson to be learned through failures. For one: it causes you to take inventories of your senses and ideals. Causes you to rethink the reason why you took on a certain task in the first place. There are many reasons why individuals fail; but two of the most important reasons are:

1. FLAT OUT QUITTING
2. AFRAID

Let's take a closer look at the first one and then the second.

QUITTER: The old saying that quitter never win and winner never quit is true in every aspect of life. In order to be successful in anything you must be persistent. You must take action on a consistent and persistent basis in order to succeed. In life there are roadblocks and stumbling blocks. What ever you choose to call them is OK. But one thing for sure is that they are there to challenge or discourage you. These obstacles can be a blessings or a curse, it depend heavily on you.

The lesson of successful people are all around us, all we have to do is study them. Take a look at Mr. Lincoln, Mr sanders and Mr. bell; you may want to ask yourself what did these three men and other successful men and women have in common? What special gift were they born with? Successful people are like babies. They did not come in to this world walking. Yet they learned to walk by getting up attempting and falling down. Every time they fall down they get right back up and take a few more steps and fall down again. The one thing that separate successful from unsuccessful people is that the unsuccessful people don't keep on getting back up and trying again.

Life is an on going battle for territories, you must fight for what you want to get out of life. The minute that you stop fighting for what you want out of life, life will give you what you don't want. Colonel sanders were turned down too many times to count as he travel the country trying to sell his chicken recipes. Just look at what his persistence done for him today. He actively began franchising his chicken business at the age of sixty-five. His father died when he was six year old. The colonel mother was forced to go out and work, so he was left to take care of his younger brother and sister. So he has to learn to cook at an early age. Even colonel sanders just didn't jump into the chicken business. He first held a series of jobs. He once was a railroad fireman. He studied law by correspondence practiced justice of the peace courts. Sold insurance, operated an Ohio river boat ferry and sold tires , even work at a service station. It was here at the service station that he began cooking for hungry travelers who stopped by. As more people started coming just for the foods, he moved across the street to a motel and restaurant that seated 142 people. Over nine years, he perfected his secret blend of spices and herbs and the basic cooking technique that is still used today. He may be gone but his legacy live on.

Last week my wife had what doctors call a light stroke,. To me there is no such thing as a light stroke. Anything that threaten my life or someone else life is serious. I'm trying to push her as much as possible; but the recovery period depends on her mental attitude more so than anything else. There will always be roadblocks in your life, but there is no roadblock bigger than the ones that you put on yourself. At this point if she just give up and quit she may never walk or speak normal again. Take something as simple as going to high school, what happen if you just decide to quit? One of the consequences of quitting would be that you would not graduate-no high school diploma. Many will agree with me when I say that there is a direct co-relationship to education and money. The more you learn, the more you can earn. Kids who don't learn to read and write earn substantially less income and have a much greater chance of ending up in prison than do their peers. Learning can be difficult at times, but you must not give up nor give in to obstacles that tried to force you to quit. Someone once told Mr. Alexander Graham Bell concerning his telephone demonstration;

"that's an amazing invention", but who would ever want to see or use one of them? People did see and did use his invention. As exciting and significant his invention was nothing compared to the litigation proceeding 17 months after Bell patent. The Bell Company was involved in 587 lawsuits, of which five went to the supreme court; Bell won every case.

PEOPLE ARE AFRAID OF SUCCESS. The magic word here is **FEAR.** Just what is fear? Fear come in two form; healthy fear and unhealthy fear. Most of our fears are just "delusion", which are distorted ways of looking at ourselves and the world around us. If we practice self-talk or others affirmations we could reduce or maybe eliminate these delusions, the source of all of our fear-healthy and unhealthy—is eradicated. Fear is one of the greatest single barriers to success in our personal and professional lives.

The reason for most people's fears is buried deep within themselves. No matter how successful we are , you must tackle fear head on, because it will not completely go away. Only you can turn your fears into power and actions. Thinking positively and feeling good about ourselves is the key to overcoming our fear. Fear is a good thing it suppose to warn us of danger and to act as a cautionary devise. But that fear shouldn't control our thoughts or what we want to achieve in our lives. It should make us stop and think before we take action. I once heard that we were born with two fears; the fear of falling down and the fear of loud noises. Once we started walking, those fears should have going away, and other fears take their places. These are the fear that someone else created for us. We only have ourselves to blame for them especially if we are allowing them to control our lives. Many people have the fear of failing. I have failed many times and I'll learned that nothing bad that I couldn't fix or work around ever happen. In fact I got one of life greatest lessons, "quitters never win, and winners never quit".

We all were born to win, but to become a winner, you must prepare to win, you must plan to win and you must expect to win. I was doing a spotlight in out local newspaper some years ago, and I was asked who was my favorite politicians and why? Abraham Lincoln was my response; and this is why; wasn't so much that he help to free the slaves, but that he had the good sense to know that a house could not stand to be divided and neither could this country. When people all around him were sticking needles and knives in every part of his body that they could find, he done something that just took nerve of steel. When Mr. Lincoln chose men for his cabinet, he wasn't too concern about his enemy. He was more concern with having a balanced cabinet of competent men. As a matter of fact he went out of his way to ensure that he got the best man for the job even if it meant mixing a group of men who had serious objections to him or to each others. Consider what he supposedly said according to historian Philip Vanderbilt Stern. "when he was thinking of using Salmon Chase in his cabinet, a friend in Springfield had warned him that Chase considered himself a bigger man than Lincoln. Well, said Lincoln, if you know of any other men who think they are bigger than I am, let me know. I want to put them all in my cabinet".

LOVE

LOVE: Men and women, we must stop using the old worn out excuse that because our father or mother never said I love you or showed affection for the family, when you were growing up; give you the free hand to act in the same manner-it don't. Especially when you know how this made you feel, you got to break this cycle of not being passionate or intimate with your family. First thing first, you must realize that you have a problem relating to your family and that you are willing to change. Do you get a weird feeling when someone tried to hug or tell you that they love you? You know that you are suppose to response with something but most of the times you end up saying, me too. When you do get the nerve to say I love you to them, do you feel empty? I was in the same boat, because my father or mother was hardly around and when they did come around they never told me that they loved me; nor did I see them showing any affection for the rest of my brothers and sisters. So later on in life when someone tried to hug me, I would freeze up, or put my arms out to keep them out of my person space.

Most of the time I felt embarrass when someone asked for a hug or told me that they loved me. Before my wife and I had children, I was pretty good at providing material wealth but love and affection was something I would used to get her or some other lady in the sack. Once I had accomplish my goal and the newness wore off, and she became part of my everyday life, I didn't know what to do with her. So I began to craw fish. I couldn't look her in her eyes and tell her that I loved her nor could I hold and comfort her with affection without it seen out of place. We as men and women must first enter into counseling and find out just what love, I mean true love really is. Before you can stand in front of your pastor,

55

family, friend and God Almighty; you need to know what you are about to undertake. Nothing can stop true love. By definition, true love bears all things, believes all things, hopes all things and most of all it endures all things. While I am on the subject of love please don't forget divine love. Once men and women understand God love, that is it's constant and not intermittent. We then will be able to accept that standard for ourselves. By understanding God love we will be able to show our own love.

Most men and women love evolve around lust, rather than true love. If you find barriers such as how a person looks or what type of job or you associate money then you're not experience true love. Again before you say I do-just remember that love is easier when everyone involves is in good health, young and beautiful. What about later on in life when one or both of you get older, and become sicks with wrinkly skin and other distractions? True love grows with the struggles of life and it shows itself by how committed you are to the other person. Don't feel too bad if your father or mother did not show or teach love by setting the example for you to follow. This is something that you along must make up in your mind and heart. Your commitment to love your wife or husband, then no matter what else is needed it will be done.

Are you willing to die for your wife or husband? Can you say in your heart that no part of your life is more important than your commitment to care for your wife or husband? If your answer is yes then you are ready. If your answer is no, then you need to seek God for his love to shine through your life and intro the life of your spouse. When you get marriage there is no such thing as a perfect love, if this what's you believe or been waiting on then you will be greatly disappointed.

FOR MEN ONLY

A MAN ROLE IN THE FAMILY

Some of the responsibilities that men have in a family are loving, leadership, provider and protector. But in order to understand man's role in the family we must go to the book of Genesis. After God made the beast of the earth after his kind: and God saw that it was good he made man. God gave man dominion over the fish of the sea, and over the fowl of the air, and over every living thing that moved. God took man and put him in the Garden Of Eden to dress it and to keep it. God commanded the man of which tree he could freely eat and which tree not to eat of, and God said, it is not good that man shall be along; I will make him a helper mate.

Out of the ground God formed every beast of the field and every fowl of the air; and brought them to the man to see what he would call them. After man named them not one could be found to be a suitable helper for him, so God caused a deep sleep to fall upon the man, and took one of his ribs and made woman and brought her unto the man. And the man said this is now bone of my bone, and flesh of my flesh: she shall be called woman, because she was taking out of man. This is why a man shall leave his father and mother, and shall cleave unto his wife: and they shall be one flesh. In the beginning both were naked but there was no naked but there was no evil thought, there was no such thing as a perverse sexual attitude. Yet out of this beautiful union there was a leader and a follow. But there was this glorious oneness in the woman.

The woman submissiveness was willing and beautiful. The man's provision was willing and beautiful. So there was no animosity, there was no struggle, there was no fighting. But from the beginning man had the role of the headship. And woman had the role of the one for whom that headship was provided. The man was the one who protected, provided, preserved and cared for the woman, who was a fitting or suitable helper for the man. After all is done and said, if you are to have a successful marriage, one that works; we need to go back where women were characterized by submission and men were characterized by sacrificial love, just like it was before the fall. When woman and man ate of the tree of good and evil, there was a curse put on every marriages. And that is why we have problem upon problems in our marriages today. We are dealing with two people who are sinful and depravity will manifest itself in the woman by seeking to overrule the man and the man buy crushing the woman without love.

FOR MEN ONLY

LOVE YOUR WIFE UNCONDITIONALLY

Many of us say concerning our imperfection, that this is the way I am; take it or leave it, I can't change, this is who I am. Bottom line, you are saying no-matter what, "I won't change". There are those of us who really are convinced that we are living our lives according to God"s words; most of the times we are wrong. Some of you know that you are not living according to God's words some of you don;t care to find out what his words say. Because of pride in our self it difficult for us to see beyond ourselves. Just take a look sometimes, I mean really take a long good look at you and your family situation. To really appreciate what you are looking at, you need to get above this earthly world and then look back down on your life and take inventories. What is your action? How is it affecting you and your family? Tell me do you like what you see? If you don't like what you see, and you really want to have a successful family life, read on. I believe that God designed marriage so we could better understand his glorious truth, this is his way of having an organized society, happy children and all around wonderful relationship for men, more important marriages is a way for God to fully reveal his love on earth.

Marriages is a great mystery no-one fully understand this, but God. God instruction to man concerning marriage is for us to love our wife. Read Ephesian 5:23. the bible go on to say, "by you husbands loving your wives the marriages might be sanctify and cleaned by the word. The bible also said that if you love yourself then you will love your wife. I don't believe that any man hate himself instead he cherish himself, no matter what. God love you so much that no matter what you do, he still love you. This is characterized as unconditional love. This is the type of love that you have for your self. It is the same love that you must have for your wife in order to have a successful marriage. The thing that you need to understand about God's love is that he is God, he made us, and so we do not deserve his love. Our wives makes us angry a lots and most of the times we respond in a negative way. A woman is a beautiful human being, she's like a computer nobody really understand her but the person who made her. What ever you put into her you can get out of her. What ever you tell her whether you remember it of not she still remember it. When dealing with her choose your words carefully especially if you are angry. I'm telling you this because there will be a time when she will play those same words back for you word by word, maybe a day, a month or years later.

Men some of us should be ashamed or ourselves, women are already grown and we cannot raise them anymore, especially not by slapping or beating on them. Many times why hanging out with the boys we think because our wives are not around she don't know what's going on. Some of us go home drunk and high after being out until two and four in the morning and jump on our wives just because she question us about where we been. We even get angry because they won't let us have sex with them because they know that we'll not going to make love to them, we just want to hit it and go to sleep. Most of the times we come home upset because we didn't get to make love to some other fine young thing while we was out. So we go into a rage when we get turned down at home too. But guess what if this is what we are doing, we don't have a home and we are too thick headed to know any better. Some of our excuses for mistreating our wives are: they don't clean up the house, they don't cook, they don't look like they did when I first marriage her, she's sick or I'm just tired of the same old stuff.

What ever the reason men, most of the times it is our fault. Don't you know that it is our job to build up our women and keep their self-esteem high? The wrong man can mess up a good woman for life. But the right man will never miss a day without showing some type of affection for his woman. Telling her how beautiful she look or smell. Taking the time out just to hold her and look into her eyes and tell her that he love her for all she do, no matter what he will always love her and be there for her, Better yet. Just ask her how was her day, sat and listen to her. Find out if there is anything that you can do for her. What the heck? Bring somethings home, or take her out, cook for her or just rub her back every other week or so just to show her how special she is to you. No matter how angry she make you feel at time. love her unconditionally, you and your marriage will be blessed for it.

FOR WOMEN ONLY

THE WOMAN JOB IN THE HOME

I know that this is a very touchy subject; and many people are more likely to talk about the death of their mother or father-in-law then to face this conversation. Our society has been struggling with this conservatively subject for a long time. Some things that a woman must be and do are:

1. Become a God fearing woman.
2. Obey your husband.
3. Become a wise woman.

No matter how smart or good you are if you don't do number one, then the rest doesn't matter no way. If you are a God fearing woman then you shouldn't have a problem with the other two. I know that many of you are thinking that I have lost my mind, old fashion or just a plain old fool. My wife often rebel when I say these things to her too. Her first question to me is what if the man is not doing those things that a husband supposed to be doing? My answer to her is;

1. Two wrong doesn't make a right.
2. Don't let some-one else make you do wrong.
3. No matter what happen, you continue to do the things that you as a wife suppose to do.
4. Let God take care of people who just don't want to do right; don't you become their judge and jurors.

These things are hard to do because they are right and just. And the society that we live in dictates otherwise. Beside it's too easy to do wrong; this is the reason why many people of this world is in the condition that they are in. Don't follow the crowds, don't become a conformity just because every body else is doing it. If you are to be a wise woman and this is what every woman should be striving to become; then you must go against the grain. Reprogram your mind to do what's right and just no matter what. If you know right, then do right, if you don't know what right look like, read the bible for your self and go to church for more than just lip services and gathering.

BECOME A GOD FEARING WOMAN: The first step in becoming wise is for you to fear the Lord our God. If you will do just this first step, then you have laid the foundation for everything else. If you fear God then you will not lie down and open your legs for the first guy who tell you how beautiful and fine you are, and how much he need and love you. A God fearing woman will wait until she is marriage. Women if you are good enough to go to bed with, then you are good enough to marriage. If he say that you all have not been together long enough to get marriage, then guess what-you all have not been together long enough to engage in sexual activities either. This may sound old fashion to you but it the way marriages was intended to be. Do you realize that here in the United States, finding a virgin at the age of twenty-three is like finding a needle in a hay stack. Anytime you go against nature, you're setting yourself up for failure. You must learn this, and teach your children the same. If you do, there will be no need for birth control pills, unless you have a life threaten illness or something that could harm you if you got pregnant.

WOMEN LISTEN UP; I cannot prove this, I am not a doctor or lawyer, but I believe that there is a direct relationship between illness and birth control. Whether you take the pill or have some type of operation that stop you from having kids, it just not natural. You are going against one of God purpose when you decide to kill your babies or just stop having babies. To kill or stop because you don't want to have anymore and you think that, this is all to it. Then you sit back and wonder why you just had a stroke or why you always in pain. Show me a woman who decided on her own to kill or stop having children, and I will show you a woman who is living with sickness and pain until the day she died.

YOUR HUSBAND AND YOUR CHILDREN: Many of you will rebel against your husband just because he's your husband. He can tell you something, saying it over and over again, but you won't believe him because he is your husband and you don't want him to be right. A stranger can come along and tell you the same thing that your husband been telling you for years. Then and only then will you believe your husband, and then you don't won't to give him the credit. You rather follow some quack on the TV or Internet first, before you follow your husband. When you are angry with your husband you go and confided in your children. You will feed them before you feed your husband. Your kids can run right over you and you will say the same things over and over again, stop this or stop that, sometimes breaking down crying. But your husband open his mouth and say to you what you know is right, yet you will slap back with your slashing tongue, throwing everything but the kitchen sink. You must stop this nonsense. When you got marriage you promise to take care of and obey your husband until death do you part. You all are no more two but one. What you do to him, you are doing it to your self. The blessing that you're be seeking, will never come. Don't choose your children over your husband. Don't love either less but more. Your children will grow up and leave you, but your husband will remain with you.

STOP THE NONSENSE with all of these Stepfather if your child daddy is alive then you all should be together. Like I said early, before you lie down and open your leg and give him the most precious jewel you have to give, get marriage first. If you are good enough to be made love to, you are good enough to marriage first. If the man want marriage you first, then don't give into his sexual desires. Don't believe the promise that if you give him your body he will marriage you later. Why would he buy a cow if he could get the milk free? God knows your heart, he knows your needs, pray to him and remain sexual free until he send you a man that will understand and marriage you first. you have to understand that many of the high and so-called power people that run this country is unsaved. Many goes to church, speak good things in church, yet these same folks will set up and pass laws design to take God out of everything, not realizing that once you take God out, you just took yourself out. Some of these laws makes divorcing your husband a win win thing for women. Yes you'll get the car, the house, the kids and his money to take care of you and the kids for a long time. It looks good on the outside, but on the inside Satan is accomplishing his goal, by tearing down the marriage institutions.

Now-a-days you have more people then ever in the history of these United States divorced or unmarried. Ladies I'm not trying to put you down cause many of you do good with what you have to work with. But it hard to raise kids by yourself, it not God's plain. Some of you are saying, a person can be marriage for a hundred years and still get a divorce. I'm saying to you that a person can be a preacher and God fearing all of his life and right before he die, lose his soul and go to hell. If something is not done to put us on the right track, we will have half of the population in prison and the other half guarding them.

LADIES, our society starts and ends with you. You can make a man bed hard or soft. You can decide just what types of children you want to raise or you can just let them or the world raise them, but to do it right , you need a husband. Believe it or not ladies, you have within you the power to decide just what type of husband you want to have. I will talk to you more on this subject later on. Some of you, get so angry with your husbands or boyfriends, that when you all do get a divorce or break up and your ex is paying child support you still have a problem letting him see little Johnny or Susan. When they get too grown for you to handle then you want their daddy to come in and get them, it's too late. You have spoiled little Johnny and Susan they're almost grown. You have different men running in and out of your children life, this not raising your children this is child abuse. You should be made to pay a fine, and if you want stop, be sent to jail. There are a few good Stepfathers out there but for the most part many are not emotionally stable enough to raise a stepchild or stepchildren. If the man not taking care of his own; what make you think that he's going to treat yours any differently? Most of the times when you get involved with a Stepfather , you are putting your kids at risk. There are biological Fathers who will violate their own children. Just imagine what is going through the stepfathers mind when you women make him angry and tell him right in front of your kids that he is not their real father. What do you think is going through his mind when your too hot, too fast, teenage daughter is walking through the house with hardly any thing on or her clothes so tight, you can see every curves? How many times have you set down with your daughters and explain to her how she should act in front of a man, what to do if someone tried to hit on her?

How many of you let them watch whatever they want to watch on TV? How many of you have had your child or children walk in on you while you all were making love? How often do you go to the school just to see what's going on inside of the classroom? Stop giving into your kids trying to buy their love. Stop buying two hundred dollars gym shoes when they want even mind you, still bring in bad grades and skipping school. Just like I said about men being unstable, guess what ladies? Many of you are unstable too. You have let some man knock you up side the head so many times, that you couldn't recognize a good man if he was standing right next to you. Then when some of you do get a good man, you think that he is weak just because he don't cuss, fuss or go upside your head. You start abusing him.

Then there are you who so mess up that you have turn away from men altogether. You're loving on other women, if it won't produce life it is wrong. Just what is this all about anyway? God didn't make Eve for Jane or Adam for Paul it is abomination to the Kingdom Of Heaven. You are going against nature, and I don't care how much money or power you may have, wrong is wrong and right is right. If you think that you have so much power, when you sat down to eat tonight and a fly or something smaller than a fly take some food off your plate, make it bring the food back. On that subject let me leave you with this; God is willing, ready and able to mend broken heart and confused minds. He will forgive you for whatever you have done wrong all you have to do is turn to him and he will bring about a change in your life.

RESPECT YOURSELF: Ladies if you don't respect your self, your kids, husbands or nobody else will either, stop telling or hollowing and cussing at your kids. Tell them what you mean and mean what you say. If they want mind you, how on earth do you expect them to mind or have respect for anyone else? By cussing at them, that is how they learn how to do it so well. Learn to close your mouth sometimes and open your ears. Listen to your husbands and don't be so quick to speak, think first. Some of you are so quick to speak that you answer a question that the man hadn't even thought of yet. By the same token don't take no put down or abuse from him either. If he needs to put his hand on you, then you need to help him change his mind ,quick, fast and in a hurry. A woman suppose to reflex tenderness, love, compassionate and beautiful. When people walk into your house they should see a home. Your present should be seen and felt throughout the house. When they see your husbands or kids; they should see you in them.

I noticed that when women first start dating a man they will buy clothes and other nice things for him, then as soon as the relationships get older or they feel comfort they stop buying him anything. You can always tell when a woman begins to feel comfort; she will walk around the house all day long in her sleep ware. At first you couldn't catch her dead in it. She was always well groomed and looking good. Now little by little her bad habits begin to show. They stop caring what they put on, unless they are going out somewhere. Let me ask this question, if you are guilt of this type of action who are you dressing for? Who are you trying to impress? If you are walking around the house dress and looking like you are having a bad hair day and as soon as you get ready to go out or somebody call and say they're coming over, you run and start putting on clothes and fixing yourself up. Who are you trying to impress? If you are trying to impress someone else on the outside you are wrong. The person you should bed trying to impress live right there in the house with you. Always keep your self up. I know that you are marriage to that man but stop taking him for granted. Yes you are taking him for grant, cause you believe that just because you have paper on him and a ring on your finger, you can walk around the house looking anyway you please. It not right but this is one of the reason why husbands cheat. If you're just shacking up with somebody,well most of the times the cheating is going to come anyway because you both are illegal, there is nothing binding you all together, you're both free to do whatever you would like to do. Some of you allow your husbands to see you at your worst and you're not even sick, it was because you were too lazy to get up and fix your self up.

This will properly make some of you angry, when I say this, but you should dress for your husbands each and every day, just like you did when you first start dating him. What many of you don't understand about a man is that a man eyes is his enemy. If it looks good then it must be good. If you feed, wash and cook for a man then he feel that this is love or you care for him. So when you all dress according to how you feel, then when your man make you angry, you stop cooking and cleaning for him, all you are doing is putting woods on a fire. You're pushing him out the door. If things are not going well at your household start by looking at and if needed changing your habits, by start dressing and looking good every day. When your man stay out all night don't say bad thing to him but do later on sat down and talk to him. Tell him that you love him and you don't like it when he stay out after a certain time. Talk to him about the both of you setting down and talking with a pastor or some other marriage professionals if needed. Throughout all of what you go through, be strong, be true to God and yourself but don't let him or no-one else take advances of you and by no mean, ever, ever take abuse, neither mentally nor physically from him.

GET YOUR HUSBAND TO DO WHAT YOU WANT HIM TO DO:

I know that some of you are laughing , but it is true you can get your man to do what you want him to do. The wife is the biggest influence on her husband then anyone else. If not then something is mightily wrong. Become a wise woman and make your husband your best friend. Just think you marriage for life right? So why not make him your best friend? It to your advance. If you are living in poverty and misery is all around, you the wife hold the key to changing all of that through your husband. Like I said early nobody has or should have more influence on the husband then the wife. But in order to enjoy the fruit's the wife has to build up the relationship with her husband. Think on this for a moment, out of all the women he knows he choice to marriage you. If your relationship is base upon fault-finding nagging and jealously you will forever live in misery and be without.

If you do nothing else all day, take just one hour each and every day and sat down with your husband and brainstorm with him. Build him up if needed, (build up his ego) and make him feel that he is the most important person in your life at that time. If you will do this in short time you will see the changes in your husband. But you got to let him know that you believe in him that there are no limitation that with God help that he can't do. Let him know there no need to be afraid of falling down on his dreams because you will be there to pick him up. Just like our body need foods so does the mind , feed him health foods and I guarantee you a life of opulency.

SUCCESS AND HEALTH

What is success if you don't have good health? All of the money and love in the world hardly mean diddle if you don't have good health. Just grab the attention of the first serious ill millionaire you run into and ask him or her what they would give if you could guarantee them good health. They would proudly turn over their fortune if you could do this. I believe that it was Moses the man of god who said that the days of man is at least three score years and ten and possible fourscore. But it was Mr. Shakespeare in Macbeth who said: "three score and ten I can remember well; within the volume of which I have seen, hours dreadful and things strange; but this sore night hath trifled former knowing." even Shakespeare read and used lines from the bible but never acknowledges it in any of his plays. The important thing here is the threescore and ten years that was promise; and the question is how do you want to live the time that God gave you here on earth? You have in your power the will to shorten or stretch this time frame. You have the power to live energetic or sick and feverishly the choice is your. To live a successful healthy life you need to pay close attention to your body needs in these areas:

1. WATER
2. SLEEP & REST
3. LIVING FOODS
4. EXERCISE
5. DETOXIFICATION
6. NUTRITIONAL SUPPLEMENTS
7. HANDLING STRESS

I call these the **SEVEN PILLAR OF LIFE** because if you do the right things concerning them they will give you opulent health, and this is what we all want including millionaires. You have to do more than just want good health you have to put work and time into it. Do you realize that your body is the Temple Of God and that the Spirit Of God dwells in you? If anyone defiles the Temple Of God, God will destroy him: for the Temple Of God is Holy, which Temple are you? **1 Corinthians 3:16, 17.** Your body is not your to do as you please. You wouldn't go and throw trash all over the church floor would you? Neither should you make yourself sick by abusing your body, which is God Living Temple.

WATER

This is the first pillar of life, and everybody knows it important in sustaining life, yet most people paid little attention until it is or almost too late. Every system in your body depends on water. Water makes up about 60% of your body weight. Water flushes toxins out of vital organs, carries nutrients to your cells and provides a moist environment for your ear, nose and tissues. Next to oxygen, water is the most important nutrient you can give your bodies. You may be able to survive for weeks without food, but you're only live days without water. Don't ever make the mistake of thinking because you consume coffee, tea, soft drinks and other beverages that are water based that they can take the place of water. Often times these beverages dehydrate your system instead of hydrating. As we age, we lose ten percents or more of our body fluid anyway. We make this process worth by drinking coffee and alcohol, we are more likely to age prematurely.

Some other reasons for drinking water are:

1. Better skin; water moisturizes the skin from the inside.
2. Lose weight; water consumption help control your weight by making you feel full so that you're eat less.
3. Flush toxins, toxins, proper intake of water lessen the work load on your kidneys and liver.
4. Cushion and lube your joints and muscles; water makes up a large part of the fluids that lubricate and cushion your joints and muscles.

5. Keep you regular; water adds fluid to your colon makes your bowel movements softer and easier to pass and help prevent constipation.
6. Control fever; water can help control fever when you are sick, it replaces lost fluids.
7. Help in perspiration; when you sweat this is your body way of controlling and regulating it temperature.

How much water do you need to drink?

Many factors influence your water needs such as:

1. How active you are?
2. What climate do you live in?
3. What is the condition of your present health?
4. Are you pregnancy or breast feeding?

The best answer I can give you is under normal condition divide your body weight by two; this is the amount of water you need in ounces.

How safe is bottle water?

The answer to this question depends on who and what they use to make the plastic bottles; and where do they get the water from. In 1998 Dr. Patricia Hunt of Case Western University in Ohio discovered that plastic made from polycarbonate can leak biphenyl (BPA) a patent hormone disruptor. BPA is a chemical found in epoxy resin and polycarbonate plastic. May impair the reproductive organs and have adverse effect on tumors, breast tissues development and prostate development by reducing sperm count. BPA can also be leached into the water bottle content through normal wear and tear, exposure to heat and cleaning agents. This includes leaving your plastic water bottle in your car during errands over a period of time.

How safe is your tap water?

If you compare the United States water to other countries then I would say yes, we have some of the best water system in the world. On the flip side of this coin, our company must comply with EPA's standard on approximately 80% of the most harmful diseases causing microbes and synthetic industrial material. There are many traces of contaminates in our tap water, but according to EPA standard they pose no significant health threat.

Should you boil your tap water?

Yes if this water going to be used for brushing your teeth or consumption in order to kill microbial and other pathogens contamination that might have escape normal water treatment. Before boiling your tap water it should be tested for high nitrate and lead level. Boiling water contaminated with nitrate and lead most often increase the concentration and potential risk.

What is the best water to drink?

Good water depend on it **ph level. PH** is the abbreviation for potential hydrogen. The higher the **ph** reading the more alkaline and oxygen rich the water is. The lower the **ph** reading, the more acidic and oxygen deprived the water. The **ph** range is from **0** to **14**, with **7.0** being neutral. Anything above **7.0** is alkaline. Anything below **7.0** is considered acidic. Human blood stays in a **ph** range around **(7.35-7.45)** below or above this range spell trouble for symptoms and diseases. Blood below **6.8** or higher then **7.8** your cells will stop functioning and you will die. No matter what type of modality you choose to use to take care of your medical problems. It won't be effective until your **ph** level is up. Your body **ph** level affects everything. One thing for sure is that diseases cannot survive in an alkaline state, but they thrive in an acidic environment. If you can manipulate the **ph level and oxygen** you may be able to reverse cancer. Lack of oxygen and the **ph** level are the two most important factors in cancer patients. Cancer needs an acid and low oxygen environment to survive and flourish within. Drinking high **ph** alkaline natural spring or mineral water can help balance your **ph** level.

SLEEP & REST

Getting adequate amount of sleep and make sure you rest while you are asleep.

Getting at least seven to eight hours of sleep each night, promotes good health and all around well being. You already know some ways that not getting enough sleep can affect you. Have you ever paid much attention to your emotions when you haven't gotten enough sleep? If you do, you will find that it didn't take much for you to get upset. Your behavior, moods, your ability too make decisions, and even your eating habits are affected by the quality of sleep we get or don't get. Many people experience frequent problems that interfere with their work. If we don't get the problem in check we can have a break down of the body immune system which causes many more health problems. It been said that people who are having trouble grasping new information or leaving new skills are told to go home and "sleep on it." the truth is you can learn better if you are well rested. Getting a good night sleep help you to remember what you have already learned. No-one can exactly say what happens during sleep to improve our learning. I once read that sleep form or reinforce the pathways of brain cells needed to perform certain tasks. I guess that it the same reason that not enough sleep causes your thinking processes to slow down. We all have experience our reaction ability slowing down because of lack of sleep.

What is the different between a person who is drunk and a person that have been deprived of sleep? The answer is not much, you see both are equally unfit to operate a motor vehicle. For years doctors have known how important sleep is for overall health and for physical and mental performance during waking hours. Everybody needs sleep to live, many things happens in our brain and body when we sleep. For one, it the brain and body time for rejuvenation. To be at your best, get a health amount of sleep and rest. Go to sleep and awake around the same time at night and morning, that way your body will let you know when it times for sleep and rest even if you forget. Remember you can't enjoy success if you're not around. The way to not be a part of this world is to stop getting your proper share of sleep.

LIVING FOODS

Living foods is food that provides enzymes, vitamins and minerals that the body needs for healing and maintaining optimal health. A lock of enzymes is a contributing factor to most health problems. Just as I explain early concerning water, when toxic and deficient conditions are removed from the body, the body can heal itself, fight o ff other sickness and then you will find success in health.

WHAT ARE SOME LIVING FOODS?

Fruits, vegetables, nuts and seeds are all living foods. I once heard a certain speaker say that we human dig our graves with our teeth. I guess it must be true because despite all of the advancements, man have made in fighting diseases, we still contract and spread diseases at an alarming rate. We have digestive problems and other ailments because we eat everything on God green earth, even things we have no business eaten. Most foods we eat have no nutritional values what-so-ever. I read an article by Brenda Cobb; she asked the question what are we really eating? In her article she mention hybridization, genetic processed, waxed, sprayed, chemically, colored, preserved, cooked, canned, frozen and even genetically altered foods, have you ever wondering why a young boy wear a size thirteen shoes when both of his parents wearing size seven and nine respectively. Back in the days when I was a hog farmer in Inverness, Mississippi it would take me seven to eight month to get a pig to a two hundred pounds hog. I understand that farmer have cut that time in half. I wonder what are they feeding the hog and us too since we eat the hog after it been killed. The chicken farms have chicken that lay more eggs a day then the chicken I had laid in a week. Imagine what they are feeding them, and again, us too. That some powerful chemical I just wonder what type of harm is it doing to us. Out of not wanted to sound like I am preaching to you; I will leave you with this . . ."If you want to have success in health then you need to eat to live rather then dying to eat".

EXERCISE FOR YOUR GOOD HEALTH

"If you don't use it or abuse it; you will lose it".

It seen that every year around January millions of you makes a New Year Resolution of getting back into shape. Things goes pretty good for the first couple of weeks and then we start lacking off until finally you just give up all together. Many times we put too much pressures on ourselves by not setting realistic goals. Some of you don't set goals at all. Either way you run out of gas within a short time. A friend of mind told me that if she could stop watching the scale she might be able to do a better job of staying with the program. We all ch testify to that. Once we have has a coupe of good days of working out the first thing we do is run to the old scale just to see how much we have lost. Then we get disappointed because we didn't lose enough or some times we have even gain a little.

Women you all have it the worse. Most of you are so self-conscious concerning your body that the least little thing turn you up side down. Before even beginning an exercising program learn to love your self first, and get to know who you are. Love your self enough to know that you have the power to transform your body to any condition that you so wishes. No matter what conditions or how old you are. It up to you if you want to stay that way or if you want to get that shape or size you once had. Just make sure before you begin any exercising or dieting program, get with your family doctor. He or she will be happy to assist you with your goals.

Exercise is a major factor for long-term weight loss. Take a person who just lose weight by dieting along will often lose the weight, but the muscle loss lowers metabolic rate and thus increases the chances of regaining the weight. You want to do somethings that will change the body's chemistry and at the same time build muscle mass. One of the greatest advantages of exercising is that it affects many hormonal systems in the body. Your body cells responsiveness increase to insulin so that the insulin does not cause increase fat storage. When you exercise your brain secrete endorphins which give you a feeling of well-being. No matter how you look at it, there is no alternative to a sound exercise program for burning fat. If your goal is to lose weight then you must include a good exercise program. To have a health body you must treat exercise just as you would treat foods. Exercising prolong your life. Without it your body will deteriorate more faster.

Exercising is a way to insure that when you reaches mid-age you will still have strong bones to support your frame and firm muscles to protect your internal organs. When you exercise, you can feel the effects throughout the body, every cell, organ and tissue reap the benefits. A vigorously exercise take oxygen to every cell of the body. Your circulation improve. You want feel as fatigue because it create energy and increase your capacity to handling stress. There have been many studies conducted concerning exercises both pro's and con's. I will only tell you the pro's here and it just because I personally don't know of any disadvantages of exercising. Here are some benefits:

1. **Exercise help you sleep more soundly.**
2. **Exercising greatly reduces the risk associated with heart disease.**
3. **It improve your ability to utilize sugar in your blood.**
4. **Help to prevent arthritis and joint stiffness.**
5. **Exercise help to control weight.**
6. **Exercise stimulates digestion and increases the absorption of nutrients.**
7. **It diminishes appetite, burns calories, build muscle and speed up metabolism.**
8. **May help to prolong life.**

NO PAIN, NO GAIN:

Once you been cleared by your doctor, remember the old saying "no pain, no gain". When you first start you will get a little sore but if you continue it will disappear before you realize it was gone. Start small, I mean take some baby steps first, especially if this is the first time you're exercise in a long time. Remember craw before you walk. Exercising is a personal decision; so is how hard you should work out. If you want to do it right, then your exercise should be based on your heart rate. As intensity increases, oxygen demand goes up and your heart beats a little faster. You should try to keep within a specified range (your target heart rate). You can find your target rate by doing some form of aerobic exercise for ten minutes. Check your pulse for six seconds and add a zero to the number of beats to get a count per minute. Subtract your target rate from your maximum heart rate. It should look somethings like this for a forty—five year old:

1. 220 – 45 = 175 (maximum heart rate)
2. 175 x .60 = 105 beats per minute
3. 175 x .80 = 140 beats per minute

This will put your training range between 105 and 140 beats per minute.

LISTEN TO YOUR BODY:

If you are hurting I mean really hurting and something tell you that something just not right. It doesn't hurt to cut back a little. If the pain persist or get worsen consult with your doctor. You might have to modify your program. Exercise programs must be reevaluated periodically. Maybe we're not achieving the results we had hoped for, or maybe an injury forces us to alter our routine. If you have been exercising for a while and you feel your program is no longer working, you may need to give it a boost. You can do this by adding intervals of greater intensity throughout your workout so your body can adjust to burning fat at a higher level. Or if you are a beginner, your muscles have probably lost the ability to burn fat, and when you first start out, you will be primarily burning sugar. When you first start exercising you will not be burning fat, even though you will be breathing heavily . You may also tire easily and get discouraged because you are not seen the results that you had anticipated. If you feel that you are overtired then cut back and start more slowly. The more you exercise the more energy you will have. Your health will improve, and then you will be able to tolerate just a little bit more. When you exercise there are four area of consideration you should be concerned with:

1. WARM UP
2. AEROBIC
3. STRENGTHENING
4. COOLING DOWN

Warming up is very important. If you just start exercising without warming up first, you will be shocking the body. Shocking the body can do major damages to organs, cells, muscles and tissues. To keep from injury yourself, you want to move your body gradually from a sedentary state to an exercise state. Stretching and low-impact exercises increase the body temperature, heart rate and muscle demand slowly. Stretching also create flexibility, which for many people reduce joint pain, improve posture, reduce lower-back discomfort and minimize post-exercise soreness. Just like any exercises, stretching is no different; you should seek medical advise before starting any exercise program. Stretching should be slow and deliberate to be effective. Don't jerky or move too rapid, you don't want to put too much tension on the muscle being stretched too fast.

Aerobic work-out is a must. Aerobic benefit the heart mostly. Anything that help the heart got to be good for the whole body. When doing aerobic, remember in order to get the maximum benefit out of it, you must increase your heart rate. Aerobic that doesn't increase your heart rate isn't doing you any good. Running is a good aerobic so is jumping rope. Remember that shoes and what you run or jump on does matter. To decrease injury to legs and feet, get you a good pair of running shoes and try not to run on concrete too much.

Strength training will make your body look and feel firm. Push-ups, pull-ups and weight training are very good for making your body look and feel ten to twenty years younger.

STAYING MOTIVATED:

For everyone out there who are having problem staying motivated, I just want to welcome you to the real world. We all have good days and bad days. The key thing here is "**DON'T QUIT**". When it come to exercising or anything else that benefit the body, that you are not used to, you have to reprogram the mind. So start by writing down the reason you want to start an exercise program in the first place. What do you hope to accomplish? In other word set some goals for yourself. But you must put it down on paper, it does no good if you keep it all in your head. Once you put them down on paper, read them often. Arraign your goals in short term and long term. You will get a boost of stimulation every time you accomplish one of your short term goal and before lone you will have reach your long term goal. Another way of staying motivated is to get a network started. Include your family members, friends, or co-workers. Have a little contest; build a little pot of money or anything that you all can come up with to give to the person who loses the most pounds in the shortest time. You may want to give something to someone who walked the most miles in a month the key here is to be created. Just remember it not hard setting a new year resolution to get into shape the problem come in, when you are not having fun doing what you doing. So make it enjoyable.

DON'T MAKE EXCUSES:

We all do it, but when ever I feel like not running I just tell myself that if it was easy, everybody would be doing it. In order to be successful in anything you must dare to be successful, be different, go against the grain, get out of the box way of thinking. Don't let poor weather or no-one to work out with you , stop you from reaching your goal. Be self-motivated. Don't tell yourself that I'm just too tired, or if you are a scale watcher stop sabotaging yourself. One thing for sure regular exercising can improve the way you look and feel. And we all can enjoy the boost of self-confidence that it gives. So come on, what are you waiting for? To day is the first day of the rest of your life. "**JUST DO IT**".

DETOXIFICATION

Waste in, waste out..the seven means of elimination

All of the exercising in the world want helps you if the seven means of eliminating waste from your body is not function properly. So our first step in detoxification process is to identify those organs that responsible for eliminating waste out of the body and how we can assist them in doing their jobs a little better. When this system is working properly you can and only then have good health. When we eat or drink there are many toxins present so the body have to process and eliminate these foreign substances as soon as possible. The body will recycle any toxin that it is not capable of getting rid of. The body will utilize all seven systems to try and expel this toxin from the body. If any one of these systems is compromised and not working properly all types of complication will be the result. The recycle system of the body that responsible for eliminating waste is the following:

1. COLON
2. LUNGS
3. KIDNEYS
4. LIVER
5. SKIN
6. BLOOD
7. **SYMPHATIC SYSTEM**

COLON

The colon's primary function is to absorbed water. The stood is liquidized when it enter the right side of the colon. As the material passes through the colon. Most of the liquid is absorbed. When it reaches the end of the left side the stool become harden. Like I told you early eat more living foods instead of eating a lot of dead foods there are thousand of chemical and substances in the food we eat. Living foods like fruits and vegetable have great quantities of antioxidant in them. Antioxidants is chemicals that neutralize the free radicals in these foods. Free radical is a natural byproduct of normal metabolism. The problem is that free radicals may cause damage within the body. On the other side dead foods such as animal meat do not contain these important antioxidants. The colon itself is approximately 5 feet maybe a little bit longer in certain people. The biggest concern with your colon is cancer. Cancer of the colon is a major health problem. It rate right up there with lung and breast cancer. When detected early colon cancer is the most curable. The cancer disease begins in the cells that line the colon. Most cancer of the colon began as a **POLYP. A POLYP** is a growth that occurs in the colon. The growth or fleshy tumors, are shaped like a mushroom or a dome like button that occurs on the inside lining of the colon. The sizes rang from as small as a pea to as large like a plum some have been larger. Many of these abnormal genes have more to do with certain family histories then anything else. There are others that have a lots more to do with our diet.

POLYPS CAN BE BRODEN DOWN INTO THREE CATEGORIES

1. Sporadic Polyps, occur between the ages of 40 and 60. they can take up to ten years or more before develop into a cancer.

2. Family Polyps, this is a hereditary condition in which the entire colon is infested with hundreds, even thousands of **POLYPS.** They normally began at an early age.
3. Hereditary Non-Polyps Colo rectal Cancer, this cancer is found in close blood relative relatives such as Father, Mother, Sisters, Brother, Aunts, Uncles and Children.

Our quality of health is determined by our daily choices. Not only is optimum nutrition is one of the key to real healing, but how much of these nutrients are absorbed and how well the body recycle the waste out.

DETOXIFICATION OF THE COLON:

You should start at the colon, because it is the body sewer system. When this system, break down or not working properly, the colon become clogged with debris that is toxin to the whole body. Here is a list of symptoms you may want to look out for:

1. Skin problems, rashes, boil pimples and acne-this is the body way of trying to expel the poisons through the skin.
2. Low energy, loss of vitality for no apparent reason, the poisons have reach some of the glands.
3. Bad breath and foul-smelling gas and stools-the poisons have reached the lungs.

WHY DO WE NEED TO CLEAN OUR COLON?

1. The foods we consume like red meat don't always recycle through the digestive system properly. Sometimes it becomes hard feces on the wall of the large intestine.
2. Another good reason for cleansing is to get rid of parasites. More than a billions people have **roundworms, whip worms, hookworms and some, even are infected Schismatics.**

THE LIVER

Poison in, poison out

You only have one liver, so you must do what ever you can to keep it and maintain it. Do you realize that your liver has over a hundred functions? That is a lot of work for the largest glandular organ of the body. It weight approximately three pounds. Some of the function of the liver is to break down fats, convert glucose to glycogen, and produce urea. Urea is the main substance of urine. Make certain ammo acids. Ammo acids are the the building block for proteins. The liver filter harmful substances from the blood, storage vitamins and minerals. The liver produces about eight percents of the cholesterol in your body.

CLEANSE THE LIVER

There are many good cleansing kits out there that will do a great job at clean your liver. A good recipe that is really cheap and work well is something that many of you have in your home already. Mix together the following items.

1. **Green Tea**
2. **Lemon Juice**
3. **Syrup**
4. **Cayenne pepper**
5. **Vinegar**

Try drinking this mixer for about five to seven days, you will be amazed to how you will feel. It doesn't take much, just add everything to make about a cup a day. Most people have livers that are overworked and for one reason or other it performance has slowed down. Out environmental problems are not going to go away over night. And every day we drank or eat toxins and in some form or faction we breathe toxin. This is why we need a liver that functioning properly. A properly function liver is one of the secrets of longevity.

LUNGS

Keep inhaling and exhaling for good health.

The lungs make up one of the largest organs in your body and they work with your respiratory system that allow you to take in fresh air, and get rid of carbon dioxide infected air. Your lungs from the outside are normal pink looking and a bit squishy, like a sponge. But if you smoke or inhale lots of bad chemical infected air then your lungs might be a grayish or dark brown looking with spots on them. Smoking damages the cilia in the trachea so they can no longer moved to keep dirt and other substances out of the lungs. Cigarette has a certain chemical in them that causes the walls of the delicate alveolar to break down , making it harder to breathe. Cigarette smoking can also damage some of the cells of the lungs so bad that they will go away only to be replaced by bad unhealthy cells, some maybe cancers. Your lungs are very important part of your detoxification system. If you eat the proper foods and take part in vigorous exercise your lungs will become stronger and better at supplying your body with fresh air it need to be successful at keeping your body health.

YOUR SYMPATHETHIC SYSTEM,

A very important part of your general nervous system is your sympathetic nervous system. This system is activated when our body sense danger whether it be social or physical. To get some sort of understanding about this system just think of your self-giving an ex extemporaneous talk; the first thing you will noted is your heart, it will beat faster, your blood pressure will rise. If this system over activate you could have a nervous breakdown. When our body is under some type of stress the sympathetic system goes into action. It slow down other body function so that more energy is available to handle what ever the distress is. If we react too strongly or let the small stuff pile up, we may run into many problems, some could be physical as well as psychological. Some people have experience gastrointestinal problem as well—nausea or diarrhea. Stress is a natural and important part of life. Without stress there would be no life. Be careful of too much stress. Too much stress bring on distress here are some suggestions designed to help you managed distress.

1. **Accept certain situation, stop getting upset over things that you cannot change, like someone else feeling on beliefs.**
2. **Exercise, a good exercise program will help to alleviate lots of stress.**
3. **Talk rationally to yourself. If you make a mistake don't beat your self up, use it as a learning tool, find out who problem it is whether it be yours or someone else.**
4. **Set good habits. Don't smoke, minimize your alcoholic use. Watch out for caffeine and sugar.**
5. **Talk to family or friend, they can be a good medicine sharing of deep feelings and thoughts can reduce stress.**

NUTRITIONAL SUPPLEMENTS

Everywhere you look there are people who are sick with many diseases that are preventable. The health care business is a billion dollars industry. The unnecessary medicine that they sell you is making a lots of people rich. If you notice I did say unnecessary medicine, because many of the people on medicine do not need to be on them. If they ate the proper foods, exercise and took the right nutritional supplements, they would be healthy.

WHAT MAKE NUTRITIONAL SUPPLEMENTS NECESSARY?

1. **For one, most of us are chronic poor eater.**
2. **Women over the age of forty who are suffering the effect of menopause.**
3. **If you are suffering from certain diseases that interfere with normal absorption of nutrients from your diet.**
4. **If you are pregnant or trying to get pregnant.**

5. **When you do not for the most part, prepare of cook your food properly.**
6. **After having an operation.**

SUPPLEMENT REGULATION

Choosing nutritional supplement is a serious matter because there are no FDA. Does not regulate the vitamin industry nor are there any laws that limited the serving size of the a mount of nutrients in any vitamin supplement. There are many fake vitamin supplements, as well as fake medicine, some are even poison.

NUTRITIONAL SUPPLEMENTS DEBATE

The pharmaceutical companies will not endorse nutritional supplement. For one it would cut their drugs profit in half. It funny that every time you go to the doctor; without him or her giving you a good examination, they already have prescribed for you a certain medication, this is big business. I'm not saying that all medicine is bad; something is going to happen. Kevin Trudeau in his book natural cure they don't want you to know has sold over several million copies. Whether the thing he say is true or not I don't know, but it was people like Ponce DE Leon, Sven George, Llinas Paulig, Casimin Funk and others who put vitamins on the map.

ONE OF THE MOST MISDIAGNOSED DISEASE IN THE WORLD

"THYROID"

You know, with all of the talk about being successful, I just got to talk about Thyroid Disease. Thyroid Disease is one of those diseases that is so trickly and common that not only is it misdiagnosed most of the times but it can be fatal. Although I will be talking about Thyroid here, but I want you to study and research any diseases that may come your way. And always if possible get a second, even a third opinion.

What is the Thyroid and where is it located?

The Thyroid is a small gland located below the skin and muscles at the front of the neck, about where you would tie a bow tie. It's brownish red, and it look like a butterfly's wings. It manufactures the hormones that help control metabolism and growth. This hormone is called thyroid hormone. It does this by producing a proteln called Thyroglobsilin and they attaching iodine to portions of it in order to produce the two froms of Thyroid Hornone called T-3 and T-4. These hormones have a profound effect on just about every part of your body. Hypothyroidism 2 a condition in which the cells are unable to utilize the hormones, he said, symptoms include fatigue, weakness, cold intolerance, muscle pain, depression, obesity muscle cramps, head aches, constipation, and heart disease. Hypothyroidism is a common condition, and it can be successfully treated however, because the symptoms are often subtle, or people believe their symptoms are due to stress, depression, or "getting older" or may frequently mistake for other conditions, it is not unusual for someone with hypothyroidism. This condition affects both men and women, but it is more common in woman.

Some causes of Thyroid Disease

There are a variety of factors that can contribute to the development of Thyroid problems.

» Exposure to too much radiation
» Over consumption of isoflavone, intensive
» Soy products, such as soy protein, capsules and powders
» Some drugs, such as lithium and cordarone
» Too much or too little iodine in the diet.

You have a higher risk of developing Thyroid Disease if

» You have a family member with a Thyroid Problem
» You have another Pituitary or Endoerine Disease
» You're female
» You're over 60
» You're a smoker
» You're just had a baby.

FINANCIAL 101

THE STEP BY STEP GUIDE TO GAINING CONTROL OVER YOUR MONEY THAT YOUR MOTHER AND FATHER DIDN'T TEACH YOU.

LESSON 1

PAY YOUR-SELF FIRST.

WHAT IS MONEY? All around you there are millions and millions of people living from pay check to pay check. Some don't have any money coming in at all, yet there are others who seem to have money trees that they pick off every morning. How can some people get paid million of dollars a year when others just barely getting by? People are risking their lives and the lives of their family every day to come to the united states. What do they know that we whom are born here don't know? For one anybody can earn enough money to sustain life here in the united states. Not only can you earn enough to sustain , but you can become wealth if you really want to and are willing to do what it take to get their, no matter what your race, color or ability. We all want money, but just how much do we know about this craving we call money? A long time ago there was no such thing as money; people got their clothing, food and needs by trading things. Some people were good hunter, fishermen, farmers or skilled at carpenters and potter making. A farmer may trade a cow, pig or chicken for some shoes from the shoes maker. Money can be define as any goods or token that is raised as a medium of exchange that is socially and legally accepted for payment of goods and services. But we understand money as being paper or coins known as currency with dead presidents on them. The currency called money is what divide the people of this world from the have and the have not. The more money you have the better your standard of living can be. Every body wants money, yet many of us do not understand enough about money to get it and keep it. Some of us want it so bad that we will kill, rob or steal for it.

LESSON 2

SAVING IS THE KEY TO FINANCIAL PEACE

If we are willing to risk so much for money, why don't you keep some of the money that slip through your fingers each payday? The average person that work have over a million dollars that come and go through their life time, yet most die broke or living dependent on monthly assistants from the government, most of the things we spend our money on are consider frivolity to the millionaires minded person. It amazed me to watch people who I know have a great deal of money pull out their coupons at the cash register. The long line of people behind him or her sighing, frowning and shuffle ring their feet in disbelief, yet these same folk don't have one-fourth of the money that these thrifts spenders have.

Most of us are too proud to cut coupon. My next door neighbor before he passed away told me to never pay full price for anything, that I don't have to. He said never ever buy the current year car, always wait until three or four years down the road. That same car, you will be able to buy it for almost half of what it would have cost had you bought it bring new. Most cars lose ten to fifteen percent of their valuable soon as you drive it off the lots. When my neighbor passed, his net worth was estimated in excess of ten millions dollars. You would think that a man with over ten millions dollars wouldn't have a problem spending thirty or forty thousand dollars on a bring new car, surely he deserve it. He explain to me things such as kickback, points, interests and some taxes I have never heard of. He advise me to wait at least three year after some other poor soul have paid all of the crazy taxes and interests; then go in with negotiation on my m ind and don;t be afraid to walk out if I didn't get the deal or come close to the deal that I was looking for. Shop around if you have to, but under no circumstance put yourself under something that you can't or it going to be a burden to pay off. He told me to try going through my banker or credit union rather than a deader arranged finance.

I ask my neighbor what was the real secret to his great success with money? He told me that every cent of every dollar should have a name and a place to go. He went on to explain that your money should be dissect like you do specimens in biology class. Look at your taxes, bills, foods, clothing and other expenses. All of these expenses are important in their own right. He said before you pay uncle SAM or any body else except God, "pay yourself first". I told him that I have so many bills that I couldn't afford to pay myself first. My neighbor looked me straight in the eyes as if he could see my soul and told me that he said that I must pay God first and then myself second in that order. He said that if I would change my way of thinking, I could change my life. According to him I was suffering from a perpetual poor man syndrome and if I didn't change this conception about money I will be perpetually poor. My neighbor put his hand on my shoulder and said that there a thing called a pre-tax retirement account that you can legally pay yourself before you pay uncle SAM. That day I learned it's not how much money you make, but how much you can save. If you make twenty thousand dollars a month but your bills at the end of the month is twenty thousands dollars; how much better off , are you compared to someone who only make five hundred dollars a month? So I made a promise to my self that day; I will give ten percents of every dollar I earn to the church and I will save ten percent or more for my self, and every body else will be third, fourth and so-on.

LESSON 3

BUDGET YOUR WAY TO FINANCIAL SUCCESS

These lessons looks good on paper but in reality if you are living with debts hanging over your head every day and every night it is a nightmare. Some of you are saying that you don't have enough to give to the church less along open a saving account with all of the bills you have. It simple, somebody got to wait, you only make so much money. I'm not telling you not to pay your bills, but you got to put somebody on the back burner until your money catches up to your bills. No you cannot put your self on the back burner nor can you put the church. This is the only way you are going to get your debts and your life back in order. So take out a sheet of paper or two and list all of your debts. Then arrange them by precedence, the most importantly first with number one beside it, then number two, etc. on that first sheet of paper where you have your debts listed, in the number one and number two spaces-put the church and then yourself in those spots. Put your total monthly income at the top of the page. Take ten percents of the total and put it beside the church. Take another ten percents and put it beside your name. The money beside your name is to go into a saving account, and you are not to touch it again. It much remain in there unless a matter of life or death situation arise. When you have save a little bit over a thousand dollars take the money out and open up a checking account, this will become your emergency account, remember life or death.

As you continue to deposit money into your saving account every month take two to three percents of that money and added it to your emergency funds. I know that many of you are saying that I am nuts, maybe. But one thing for sure, I'm not telling you nothing that I my self haven't done. You must have a rainy day fund set aside because as sure as the sun is shinning right now one day its going to rain, and you need to be prepared not getting prepared. That money in your saving account is not for you to spend it on a vacation or some other foolish things. You don't have enough save up yet. This money in your saving is for you to invest and grow. It is for your retirement purpose only. If you really want a vacation then save for it at the same time you are saving for retirement and keeping your emergency funds going. If you can't afford to save for retirement, emergency and a vacation too, guess which one you can't afford and have to cut lose? You're right if you said vacation. Get a second job, or do what you can to save for your vacation if it that important to you.

LESSON 4

EDUCATE YOURSELF CONCERNING MONEY

The best budget system I know today out of all the different software out there for budgeting, none come close to the envelop system. This system is based on setting down with yourself or if you are living with someone then your significant other. The two of you need to set down and do this: out of the total money you bring home a month, make a envelop for each bill or payments you need for example:

- » **Envelop for church**
- » **Envelop for saving**
- » **Home mortgage**
- » **Car payment/gas**
- » **Credit cards**
- » **Food**
- » **Clothes**
- » **Gas bill**
- » **Phone**
- » **Electricity**
- » **Miscellaneous, like eating out, going to the movies, going bowling, etc. If you don't have a budget its like driving without knowing where you are going and you don't have a road map. This is no maybe this is a much for family, if you want truly financial peace then you have to become weird and live today like no one else, so you can live tomorrow like no one else.**

LESSON 5

MOST DEBTS ARE DUMB, SO STOP THE INSANITY.

If we could become just a little bit more educated concerning our financial situation, I believe that life of abundance will be within our reach. Not known something or others, present many obstacles for us concerning our money, just because we don't understand. Once you learn how a certain thing is supposed to work and what to do if it doesn't work according to specification you are able to take some type of action. Being confused concerning your money causes you to make costly mistakes, bad financial decision or worst, do nothing at all. Our parents taught us many things whether they intended to or not. We all have a money blueprint and we inherited it from our parents.

May parents did not give me the necessary tools to build wealth but I cannot place all of the blame on them. For one, their parents did not give them the necessary information to build wealth. So we all make mistakes, accumulated credit card debts, no retirement, nothing for the future, just a lot of mess we don't really need. But until you make up your own mind about your individual knowledge concerning money and the willingness to start today learning how to attract money, keep money and grow money you will forever be without.

Women you all are in a unique financial situation just through the fact you all generally live longer than men. Because of widowhood, divorce or just never married eighty to ninety percent of all women at some point in their lives will be in charge of their own financial. So women it's high time that you start playing catch up. Don't just leave financial knowledge and investing up to men. You too need to take responsibility for your own financial security. Many of you have gone through your whole life depending on someone else to control your saving and investing so if you're middle age and never learn about money; that's bad, but it isn't the end of the world and it's not too late. You can start learning about money now and start making the right decision concerning your money and you will have a great retirement.

Remember knowledge is empowerment. The more you know the better you can prepare for the fight and over come fears. If you have internet capability, search financial websites, take as many financial classes and financial seminars as you can. Talk to people in the know, someone who is successful with their own financial may be able to guide you in the right direction. Like I said earlier, the best thing you can do is set financial goals; determine where you are today and where you want to be tomorrow. You have to get your husband involved if he's not already. If he takes care of all the financial, it's high time that you start taking and learning some of these responsibilities. Tomorrow is not promised to anyone.

LESSON 6

DEBTS IS A TOOL, IF YOU USE IT TO CREATE PROSPERITY.

Which statement is true? It depends o n who you are and how you interpret each. Both of the statements can be true, it really depend on the reader, let's take a closer look at each . . . .

DUMB DEBT

Most people are up to their nose in debts. They have so much debts that their hard earned cash is already gone before they even cash their pay checks. This is insane, you must stop living like this. As long as you have debts hanging over your head, you cannot be happy because you are a slave to who ever you owe the debt to. I might even say that they own you for a while; especially if you have to rob peter to pay Paul. Dumb debts are really when you buy things on credit that you either can't afford or you don't need. Some of us buy on credit and then start skipping payments. Just when they decided to make up the payments, some mishaps or other comes along and make them miss one or many more payments, that's causes the original debt to compound. Many of you already have bad credit, yet you fall victim to the pay day loan folks or rent to own folks. From day one, you are paying an insane amount of money on something that in the first place you don't even need and secondly you'll paying double or triple the original cost had you save up for it. I have an uncle who remain nameless goes out and buy a car that he cannot afford and four months later quick his job because the manager forced him to come in and work on one of his days off. "Bad credits and bad habits make a large pot of dumb debts".

USING DEBT TO CREATE PROSPERITY

All debts is not dumb and can be use as a tool to create prosperity, providing that the person using it understand how much he or she can handler. Good debt managements can be worth it weight in gold. Debt is good when you are buying items that you need and item that will appreciate in value instead of depreciating in valued. Many years ago, I learned how to accumulate wealth by something called the guns and butter theory. To make a long story short, each of us have a certain amount of money and credit that we spend on guns and butters items. Guns items are goods such as stocks, bonds, gold, and real estate. Butter items are classified as goods like cars, boats, stereos and fancy clothing. Simple put certain items go up in value while others lose their values. You can either have assets or liabilities. Assets put money in your pockets. Liabilities take money out of your pockets. Somewhere I read a quote that stated, "He who invests his dollars wisely in guns today will discover that tomorrow his investments will generate enough return to buy him all the butter items he will ever need or want".

Having said that, I will answer yes; debts is a tool that can be used to create prosperity. For example; if there was no such thing as credit many of us wouldn't own or have some of these fine houses we enjoy so freely today. Many of us would not have multimillion dollars business. Some people didn't have a dime to their name, but because somebody somewhere believed in them enough to let them have somethings when they didn't have anything. Many people today have gotten a house on credit and sold it for a profit many times over. Take credit cards for example they can be a blessing or a curse. You can either work for them or let them work for you. Now before you go out and get yourself some credit cards you need to educate yourself concerning how to manage your financial, if not, you will never meet a worst financial enemy then a credit cards company, seeking money that you owe other than the I. R. S.

LESSON 7

MANAGING YOUR RECORDS

Managing your records is the most single thing you can do while on your way to financial freedom. Aren't you tired of waiting until tax time just to find out that you don't know where your important papers are. There is an old saying that's say; "the job isn't completed until the paperwork is done." when it come to your financial freedom or life itself, there is a certain rhymes where everything come together. When you have to turn your house upside down every time you'll looking for important paperwork is time consuming and costing you money. By taking time out now, to organize your important paperwork and staying organized will save you lot's of headaches. There are many advances to good record keeping such as:

1. **Having information at your fingertips when you need them the most.**
2. **Keep you informed and show proof concerning when a certain payment is due and show when it was paid.**
3. **Just a way to show that you are in control of your financial life.**
4. **If you'll ever in a litigation concerning missing payments or some other mishap concerning receipt or other paperwork's.**
5. **Keeping all of your tax information in one place and up to date.**

I'll spent one half of my life in the military and have experience certain paperwork's always come up missing right around promotion time. So I went out and purchase me a filing cabinet and a computer. I copy everything in my military records and put it on the computer and a hard copies ready available in my filing cabinet. Not only was this good for my military career, but also for civilian life as well. Working in Correctional like the Mississippi State Penitentiary, Corporation Of America, Shelby County Sheriff Department, taught me that good records keeping is important to staying ahead of the game. There are hundred of things that take place in your life. Some times it is almost impossible to keep control of all the paperwork without some formal record keeping system. You will lose some of the important paperwork and end up keeping some, that should have been thrown out years ago. I know that this sound a little boring and time consuming but if you start managing your paper work properly it will become more easy as you continue to do it. It will also end frustration, time and money losses caused by lost or misplaced paper works. To get started I would go out and buy me about twenty-five or more manila file folders, and put them in two of my unused drawers. When you have more money go out and buy you a two draw filing cabinet. On each of the folders I would write a title name on it and I would placed them in alphabetically orders, for example air line would be my first folder if I like flying a lots; then

2. Bank Statements.
3. County Club.
4. Credit Bureau Report.
5. Doctor Bills.

The list goes on and on, every things that I need to keep will just be file away in one draw. I would keep every thing current for this year in the first draw and every things I need to keep permanent in another draw for as long as I need to keep it then I would discard it. I would go out and buy me a computer if I didn't already have one, and keep my records on backup disks and external hard drives. If you develop a good record k keeping system it won't be long before your friend start calling you weird and you'll began to grow in financial prosperity.

LESSON 8

INVESTING YOUR HARD EARNED DOLLARS

How comfortable are you at taking risks?

Let me be blunt, investing is about taking risks, you could lose all or some of your hard earned money, I don't want to sound dramatic but you take risks every times you drive your car, fly in an airplane, eat out or go on a vacation. When you leave your home for whatever reasons there's no guaranteed that you will ever return, so there you have it, it called life, and life is about taking risk, some of you just don't know it. But before you plunge into investing if this is the first time you ever done something like this, admit it to your self first, that you need help, and then go out and read everything you can get your hands on. Talk to people in the know who are investing their money everyday and have been doing so for years. Here are a few things that you should consider before investing:

1. **Risk; normally the greater the risk, greater the returns. Can you afford the risk, is a serious question you should ask yourself. If you are investing money that you need to live on, I will quickly tell you, no, don't do it. Money to invest with should be monies**

that you have left over after all needs have been met. In other word take care of all important matter first. Your bad habits money like smoking, drinking and gaming is great money to invest with. But before you drop one cent toward investing just make sure that you do your home work first. There are lots of scams out there that look like investments. Most of the times if something just too good to be true, it is, run away from it. You need to know if you are trying to grow your money or if you just want to have security. Some investing take many years to grow in value and doing those years some even go backwards a few times.

2. Make a plan, yes even in investing you need to have a plan. Never rush into a decision if you don't have to without making a plan first.
   » What are your goals?
   » What do you want this money for?
   » When do you want to use this money?

Because everybody has different circumstances, these questions should help you come up with a plan. Don't be afraid to ask for help if you don't know how to do somethings or others. You have experts out there who have been doing this for years. Seek them out and weight your decisions. **Remember, even the experts make bad investments decision sometimes.**

3. Time, how long are you investing for? Is this something you want to do for a short time or for the long haul? How soon do you need your money is one of the greatest question you can ask yourself before investing. If you cannot afford to tie up your money for six years or longer, then you are better off investing for the short term. Be careful if you don't have other money save up it may be very costly if you have to get to your investments money for an emergency.

4. Don't put all of your money on one stock. It hardly ever pays to have all of your eggs in one basket. DIVERSIFICATION, is the key word here and if you don't know what it means then you may want to educate yourself just a little bit more before trying

to invest. Set financial goals, determined where you are today and where you want to be tomorrow.

5. You got to get your husband or wife involved if he or she not already. If he take care of all of the financial it's high time that you start taking and learning some of these responsibility tomorrow is not promise to anyone.

LESSON 9

BANKS

What is there to say about bank? "Much."

Gone are the good old days when bank was run by local people who lived in your neighborhood. These days your local banks has been taken over by some bigger bank that properly have their corporate office out of state. The problem that I have with most people who work in the bank is that they make you feel that they are doing you a favor when you go to withdraw or make a deposit. Don't they know that if everybody start keeping their money at home of deposit their money in some other bank that they would be out of a job. I live in a small town in Mississippi and we have two banks, one of the banks gives the town a grant for over three hundred thousand dollars to rebuild some of the building in the downtown district.

Most cases grant money does not have to be paid back. This bank has been doing this for over the last five years or so. I'm thinking if this bank have that much money that it can donate and not expect a return, why do they have so many problems making loans of two to three thousand dollars to just regular citizen? If you have a checking account at your local bank and you write a check that come up a few dollars short, you would think that your bank would cover you until you could get in and pay it. For some people this is true, because they have a relationship with their banker or loan officer. You must do the same thing, and if your bank refused to call you if you come up a few dollars short then it's time for you to find you another bank to deal with. The bank will charge you approximately thirty dollars to process an insufficient funded check. Sometimes those checks are run through the system twice.

Many of you are saying that the bank is right because they should be compensated for all of the troubles it goes through to process the insufficient funded checks. Would you believe that it cost most bank just a little bit over a dollar to process this type of check? Would you also believe that the banking system make millions of dollars a year in profit just of these type of check. So to whom advantage is it to not call you up and tell you about our check that's about to bounce? All I am saying is that the bank do call certain people up and tell them about their shortcoming and at times will hold those people checks until they can come in and pay them, we are all customers. If they can do for one then they should be doing for all. Believe it or not but one bad check can be like a run away train. It can have a dominoes effect on everything else that you have in your account. One bad check can cause other checks to bounce too, especially if your bank runs that same check through twice and charges you for them.

The banks are going to get their money off top, you can believe that. All of this could have easily been handle through a friendly phone call. Better yet you as a consumer, need to take more responsibilities when it come to your money. On another note, why you are there at your local bank try to get to know them, talk to your loan officer and find out what is his or her floor limit. This is the amount of a loan that the loan officer can approve themselves. If you are going to be successful with your financial, then it is equally important for you to not only be smart about how you handle your money but also the people that you trust to handle your money for you.

LESSON 10

TEACH YOUR CHILDENS ABOUT MONEY AND CREDIT AT AN EARLY AGE

Early in one of the lesson concerning financial I told you that many people have earned hundreds of thousand of dollars and after a life of hard work the o only thing that they have to show for it is bad heath and broke. If we could just get back a fraction of the money that we have let slip through our hands, we would be well off. When we were going to school the closer I got to learning about financial was general business. It taught me nothing about money, credit and how to save. The entire classes of math like calculus, geometry and algebra does a child no good if he or she can't curb their spending. I bet that many of you right now wish that someone has taught you how to save and take care of your credits, I know I do. Don't let your children find out the hard way about how to handling money. Teach them early that way we can break this cycle of depending on the government for hand out when we don't really need them. Most of stress and anxiety in our life concerning money is our own doing, but like I always say, " if you don't know, then you don't know." But don't let that be an excuse for not learning. Debt is a social disease just like smoking or drinking. Not only will they erode your life away but your wealth as well.

1. Teach your kids that to build wealth is simple, but it does take a little time. If they start now while they are young, when they reach middle ages they should be sitting real good as financial is concerned.
2. There is nothing wrong with giving your kids an allowance but if they are old enough give them a job. Don't just give them money just because they are your kids. Let them do a little some some to earn it. this will teach them responsibility, and if they do a real good job give them a raise and explain to them why they are receiving or not receiving a raise.
3. Opening up a saving account in your child name is a great learning tool to teach responsibility. As they grow older teach them about other money matters that they can invest their money in and not just an saving account but mutual funds, Ira's and Cd's as well. But again parents you got to get off the soft and learn about these things yourself. How can you teach your children , if you do not know?

SOME PEOPLE WHO HAVE INFLUENDED ME

MAYA ANGELOU

She was born Marguerite Johnson in ST. Louis, Missouri, on April 4, 1928. She is an author, poet, historian, songwriter, play writer, dancer, stage and screen producer, director, performer, singer, and civil right activist. She is best known for her autobiographical book: All God's Children Need Traveling Shoes. The first black woman Director in Hollywood. Angelou has written produced, directed and stared in production for stage, film, and television. When she was three years old, her parents divorced and she and her four year old brother bailey were sent along by train to live with their grandmother in Stamp, Arkansas. While living with her grandmother Angelo participated in a wide variety of dance classes including tap, jazz, foxtrot, and salsa. After four years in Stamp, the children returned to their mother's care. At the age, f eight, Angelo confessed that her mothers boyfriend, Mr. freeman, had sexually abused her and Angelou uncle beat the man to death. Horrified by the outcome she became mute, believing as she has stated, the power of her words led to someone's death, she remained nearly mute for another five years, at which point her mother sent the children to live with their grandmother once again,m Angelou credit's a close friend in Stamps Mrs. flowers, for helping her "refine her voice." she began to speak again at age 13, during one of her first bouts of activism, Angelou persisted at age 15, in becoming the first black person hired on the San Francisco streetcars.

In 1940, while spending the summer with her father in the Los. Angles area, Angelou was assaulted by her father's live in girlfriend. Which led to her running away from home and spending a month as a resident of a junk yard that housed other homeless children. She finally called her mother and was sent a ticket back home to San Francisco, but her month of homelessness had a profound effect on her way of looking at the world. She says "after a month my thinking processes had so changed that I was hardly recognizable to my self, the unquestioning acceptance of my peers had dislodged the familiar insecurity, after hunting down unbroken bottles and selling them with a white girl from Missouri, a Mexican girl from Los. Angles and a black girl from Oklahoma, I was never again to sense myself solidly outside the pale of the human race. The lack of criticism evidenced by our ad hoc

**community influenced me, and set a tone of tolerance in my life."
Angelo became pregnant at the age of 16, and gave birth to her son.**

ANDREW CARNEGIE

NOVEMBER 25, 1835-AUGUST 11, 1919

Andrew Carnegie's life was a true "rags to riches" story. Born to a poor
Scottish family that immigrated to the United States, Carnegie became
a powerful businessman and a leading force in the American steel
industry. Today, he is remembered as an industrialist, millionaire, and
philanthropist; Carnegie believed that the wealth had an obligation to
give back to society. Carnegie's father, Will Carnegie, was part of a British
working class movement in Scotland which believed in making condition
better for the working man. Will Carnegie was a weaver but when he was
unable to find work in America he tried to produce and sell his own cloth,
he died at the age of 51. Andrew Carnegie's education and passion for
reading was given a great boast by Colonel James Anderson who opened
his personal library of 400 volumes to working boys each Saturday night.
Carnegie was a consistent borrower.

He was a "self-made man," in both his economic development and his
intellectual and cultural development. His capacity and willingness
for hard work, his perseverance, and his alertness, soon brought forth
opportunities. At the height of his career, he was the second-richest person
in the world, behind only John D. Rockefeller of Standard Oil. Carnegie
wrote the gospel of wealth, in which he stated his belief that the rich
should use their wealth to help enrich society. The following is taking
from one of Carnegie's memos to himself: "Man Does Not Live By Bread
Along. I have known millionaires starving for lack of the nutriment which
along can sustain all that is human in man, and I know workmen, and
many so-called poor men who revel in luxuries beyond the power of those
millionaires to reach. It is the mind that makes the body rich.

There is no class so pitiably wretched as that which possesses money and
nothing else. Money can only be the useful drudge of things immeasurably

higher then itself, exalted beyond this, as it sometimes is, it remains calibers still and still plays the beast. My aspirations take a higher flight. Mine, be it to have consulates to the enlightenment and joys of the mind, to thee things of the spirit, to all that tends to bring into the lives of the talus of Pittsburgh sweetness and light. I hold this the noblest possible use of wealth." Carnegie believed that achievement of financial success could be reduced to a simple formula, which could be duplicated by the average person, in 1908, he commissioned (at no pay) Napoleon Hill, then a Journalist, to interview more than 500 high and wealth achievers to find out the common threads of their success.

MADAM C. J. WALKER

Born Sarah Breed Love on December 23, 1867 in Delta, Louisiana. Madam C. J. Walker, was born into a former slave family to parents, Owen and Minerva Breed Love. She had one older sister, Loruvenia and brothers Alexander, James, Solomon and Owen Jr. her parents had been slaves on Robert W. Burner's Madison Parish Farm which was a battle staging area during the civil war for General Ulysses S. Grant and his union troops. She became an orphan at age 7 when her parents died during an epidemic of yellow fever. To escape the epidemic and failing cotton crops, the ten year old Sarah and her sister moved across the river to Vicksburg in 1878 and obtained work as maids. At the age of fourteen, Sarah married Mosses Mcwilliams to escape her sister's abusive husband. They had daughter Leila (later known as Aphelia Walker a central figure in the Harlem renaissance) when Leila was only two years old Williamson died. Sarah second marriage to John Davis august 11, 1894 failed and ended sometimes in 1903. she marriage for the third time in January, 1906 to newspaper sale agent Charles Joseph Walker. They divorced around 1910.

Madam Walker was an entrepreneur who built her empire developing hair products for black women. She claims to have built her company on an actual dream where a large black man appeared to her and gave her a formula for curing baldness. When confronted with the idea that she was trying to conform black women hair to that of whiter, she stressed that her products were simply an attempt to help black women take proper care of their hair and promote its growth. Her third husband, Charles Joseph Walker and her daughter Leila had key roles in the growth and day to day operations of the business. In September, 1906 Mmadam Walker and her husband toured the country promoting their products and training sales agents while Leila ran a mail order operation from Denver. From 1908 to 1910 they operated a beauty training school, the Leila College for Walker hair viticulturists, in Pittsburgh. In 1910 they moved the central operation to Indianapolis then the country's largest manufacturing base, to utilize that city's access to eight major railway systems. At this height of success madam walker gathered a group of key principals to run the company, and she and her husband divorced. She became an inspiration to many black women. Fully recognizing the power of her wealth and success she learned to promote her business which in turn empowered other women in business.

She gave lectures on black issues at conventions sponsored by powerful black institutions; she also encouraged black-Americans to support the cause of world war 1 and worked to have black veterans granted full respect. Madam Walker's home, Villa Leeward, was built in august of 1918 on Irving Ton on Hudson, New York. Her neighbors included Industrialists Jay Gould and John Rockefeller. The grand estate served not only as her home but as a conference center for summits o f race leaders to discuss current issues. Madam Walker died at Villa Leeward at the age of 51 on Sunday may 25, 1919 from complications of hypertension. Upon her death she was considered to be the wealthiest African American Woman in America and known to be the first African American woman millionaire. Some sources cite her as the first self-made American woman millionaire.

REGINALD F. LEWIS

THE WEALTHIEST BLACK MAN IN HISTORY

Reginald F. Lewis was an African American born to a working class family on December 7, 1942 in East Baltimore. He was born during a time when no one had heard of Martin Luther King Jr. civil rights, or integration. Blacks at that time could not try on clothes or shop at many downtown stored. We couldn't eat in certain restaurants or go to certain movie theaters. From his youth Mr. Lewis was known for his drive and desire for excellence. The strong work ethic from his mother and grandfather coupled with his life long hunger for wealth and personal glory fueled his success on the playing field, in the classroom and in the boardroom. In high school he earned four varsity letters in baseball, three in football where he was the starting quarterback and two varsity letters in basketball. He attended Harvard Law School and became a successful corporate lawyer before remaking himself into a financial and buyer of corporations.

He ultimately moved into the elite circle of wall street deal makers. Mr Lewis grew up to become the wealthiest black man in history and one of the most successful entrepreneurs of all times, reigning over a commercial empire that spanned four continents. From a blue collar youth on the streets of east Baltimore he propelled himself to the Harvard Club on 44th street. He was known as an iron willed negotiation and brilliant strategist in action as he finessed on phenomenal deal after another. Mr. Lewis wasn't very approachable but through expertise or influence or both he commanded respect. He was a proud fiercely determined man with a razor sharp tongue and intellect to match. He brought the McCall Patters Co for $22.5 millions, fetching a 90-1 return on his investment. While this can certain be considered a great accomplishment, his greatest accomplishment was winning the right to buy Beatrice for $1 billion. Mr. Lewis outbid several multinational companies including Citigroup, who had squads of accountants, lawyers and financial advisers.

He relied on moxie. Financial and legal savvy and the efforts of a two man team consisting of himself and a recently hired business partner. With this fete he had achieved one of the more spectacular corporate buyout in an era of such mega deals. With single mindedness of purpose Mr.

Lewis fought the odds and won. He succumbed to brain cancer in January 1993 at the age of 50. his net worth was estimated by Forbes at $400 millions putting him on the magazines 400 list of wealthiest Americans. In the last five years of his life, Mr. Lewis gave away more money than most people dream of earning in several l lifetimes and he general did so without fanfare.

OPRAH WINFREY

Born in Kosciusko, Mississippi, Oprah Winfrey was reared by her grandmother on a farm where she "began her broadcasting career," by learning to read aloud and perform recitations at the age of three. From age 6 to 13, she lived in Milwaukee with her mother. After suffering abuse and molestation, she ran away and was sent to a juvenile detention home at the age of 13, only to be denied admission because all the beds were filled. As a last resort, she was sent to Nashville to live under her father's strict discipline. Vernon Winfrey saw to it that his daughter met a midnight curfew and he required her to read a book and write a book report each week. "as strict as he was", say Oprah he had some concerns about me making the best of my life, and would not accept anything less than what he thought was my best. Oprah broadcasting career began at age 17, when she was hired by WVOL Radio in Nashville, and two years later signed on with WTVF-TV in Nashville as a reporter/anchor, she attended Tennessee State University, where she majored in speech communications and performing arts.

In 1976, she moved to Baltimore to join WJZ-TV news as a co-anchor. And in 1978, discovered her talent for h hosting talk shows when she became co-host of WJZ-TV'S "people are talking", while continuing to serve as anchor and news reporter. In January 1984, she came to Chicago to host WLS-TV'S "AM Chicago", a failing local talk show. Unless than a year, she turned "AM Chicago" into the hottest show in town. The format was soon expanded to one hour, and in September 1985 it was renamed "The Oprah Winfrey Show". Seen nationally since September 8, 1986, "The Oprah Winfrey Show", became the number one talk show in national syndication in less than a year. In June 1987, in its first year of eligibility,

"The Oprah Winfrey Show", received three daytime Emmy awards in the categories of outstanding host, outstanding talk/service program and outstanding direction. In June 1988, "The Oprah Winfrey Show", received its second consecutive daytime Emmy Award as outstanding talk/service program, and she herself received the International Radio and Television Society's "Broadcaster Of The Year", Award.

She was the youngest person and only the fifth woman ever to receive the honor in IRS's 25—years history. Before America fell in love with Oprah Winfrey the talk show host, she captured the nation's attention with her poignant portrayal of Sofia in Steven Spielberg's 1985 adaptation of Alice Walker's novel. "The Color Purple". Oprah performance earned her nominations for an Oscar and globe award in the category of best supporting actress. Critics again lauded her performance in native son, a movie adaptation or Richard Wright's classic 1940 novel. Her love of acting and her desire to bring quality entertainment projects into production prompted her to form her own production company HARPO Production Inc, in 1986. today, HARPO is a formidable force in film and television production. Based in Chicago, HARPO entertainment group includes HARPO Production Inc HARPO films and HARPO video Inc. in October, 1988, HARPO Productions Inc acquired ownership and all production responsibilities for "The Oprah Winfrey Show", from capital Cities/ABC, making Oprah Winfrey the first woman in history to own and produce her own talk show. The following year HARPO Produced it first television miniseries, The Women Of Brewster Place, with Oprah as star and executive producer. It has been followed by the TV movies "There Are No Children" (1993), and "Before Women Had Wings" (1997), which she both produced and appeared in. in 1991, motivated in part by her own memories of childhood abuse she initiated a campaign to establish a national database of convicted child abusers, and testified before a U. S. /senate Judiciary Committee on behalf of national child protection act. President Clinton signed the "Oprah Bill" into law in 1993, establishing the National Database she sought which is now available to law enforcement agencies and concerned parties across the country.

Oprah Winfrey was named one of the 100 most influential people of the 20th century by time magazine, and in 1998 received a lifetime achievement award from the national academy of television arts and sciences. Her influence extended to the publishing industry when she began an on-air book club. Oprah book club selections became instant bestseller and in 1999 she was presented with the national book foundation's 50th anniversary gold medal for her service to books and authors. She is one of the partners in oxygen media Inc. a cable channel and interactive network presenting programming designed primarily for women. In 2 000, Oprah's angel network began presenting programming a $100,000 "use your life award", to people who are using their lived to improve the lives of others. When Forbes magazine published into best of America's Billionaires for the year 2003, it disclosed that Oprah Winfrey was the first African-American Women to become a Billionaire.

SAM WALTON

Sam Walton was a man who took chances, never said never, and kept on fighting the odds. He was like no other man in the world. All through his life, he has fought an up hill battle and in the end, he won. Sam Walton was a leader not a follower. Sam Walton grew up during the depression and knew that hard work and thrift were a way of life. Sam Walton was industrious. Always trying to get the most out of money, and had a burning ambition to succeed. This is all apparent by how he helped his family through the depression. Started a business from almost nothing, and changed the field of management. Sam Walton was born on march 29, 1918 to Thomas Gibson and Nancy Lee Walton near Kingfisher, Oklahoma, where they owned and lived on a farm until 1923. the Walton has decided that the farm was not profitable enough to raise a family.

Sam younger brother Jaime's was born in 1921. dad decided he would go back to being a farm loan appraiser. Once this job started, the Walton Family moved out of Oklahoma and moved from town to town in Missouri. This would traumatize most children but for the Walton boys thought it was no big deal. When Sam was in the 8th grade at Shelby, he became the youngest boy in the state's history to become an eagle scout and this was only a start of his many accomplishments. As Sam Walton grew up, he was always an ambitious boy. He attended Hickman high school in Columbia there he played basketball and football in which he was the starting quarterback for the football team and lead them to the state title in 1935. he was not the smartest person school but he was determined to do well. He severed as vice-president of his junior class and president of the student body his senior year. Don't think this is all SAM did through, he also had to help support his family along with his father and brother, because money was lacking due to the depression. Sam's job was to milk the family cow, bottled the milk, and then take the surplus to the customers and then deliver newspaper afterward. When he graduated from high school, he was voted the "most versatile boy" in his class. During this time, it would have been easy for Sam to just give up on school and go work full time. Seeing through how his family was struggling to make ends meet. He decided he was going to stay in school and attend the university of Missouri.

At the university of Missouri Sam majored in economics. He could not really afford to attend school so he worked extra hard to get the money. Sam waited tables in exchange for meals, life guarded at the school pool, and delivered newspapers. While he was not doing that he was fraternity in which he was an officer, or at a student government meeting since he was a member of the student senate, or fulfilling his duties as an ROTC Officer. Then on Sundays he was president of a Sunday school class in which many of his fellow classmates attended. While accomplishing all this he was also in the national honor society. When Sam Walton graduated in 1940, he was voted the permanent president of this class. Three days after graduation he entered the retail world working at J C Penney's in Es Moises Iowa as a management trainee earning a salary of $75.00 a month. As Sam grew up and anyone could see how determined he was to succeed and as time passed he went from being a poor town boy to the richest man in the world. He gained experience at Penney's but in early 1942, Walton resigned to wait to be inducted into the military services for World War 11. while waiting Sam took a job in a DU Point munitions plant near Tulsa, Oklahoma.

While working and living near Tulsa, Sam met his future wife Helen Robson. She lived in a little town called Clare more where she attended Clare more high school and the University of Oklahoma at Norman and graduated with a degree in business. They met in April of 1942 and were married o n February 14, 1943. in 1944, they had their first son, Samuel

Robson (Rob). John Thomas was born in 1946, James Carr (Jim) born in 1948, and Alice born in 1949. her father was a prosperous banker and rancher who would go on to help Sam start his first store. Soon after they were married Sam went to serve in the U. S. Army Intelligence Corps in the Continental United States supervising Security at aircraft plants and prisoner of war. By the time, Sam was discharged from the war he was ranked as Captain and decided he wanted to own his own department store. This dream came a reality in the fall of 1945, when he purchased a store in Newport with the help of his father-in-law. Sam borrowed $20.000, from his father-in-law and had $5000.00 saved from the military. Sam's store was a franchisee of the Butler Brothers. Who consisted of two chains, one chain were the federated department stores, which were small department stores and then the Ben Franklin variety stores. Sam store was going to be a variety store and with the assistance of the Butler Brothers, his store led in sales and profits in the six states regions. Sam made this possible by properly stocking all the shelves with a wide range of goods with very low prices, keeping his store centrally located. It was easily accessible to many customers stayed open later than most stores especially during Christmas seasons.

He experimented with discount merchandising (buying straight from the wholesaler which enable him to lower his price per item and then was able to sell a greater quantity of goods, and thereby increasing his sales volume and profits). All these ideas were new to businesses but Sam caught on fast and was able to use them to his advantages. Since his store was such a success, everyone wanted a piece of the action. His landlord wouldn't renew his lease. Because he wanted the business for his son. Sam sold the store and made a profit over 450.000, this deal was completed in January 1951, and the new owner then took possession of the store. This did not stop Sam from continuing with his d ream, before the sale was even finalized between him and his landlord Sam started looking for a new place in town but he would have no such luck, in 1850 through, he purchased a store in Benton ville, Arkansas which ended up being called Walton's five and dimes. This store was also a member of the Butler Brothers Ben Franklin chain.

Before this store opened, it needed many improvements but to Sam, that was no problem. He was never discouraged for a second. To introduce his store to the new town in July 1950, Walton staged his first sales promotion called the "remodeling sale", and then the following March he had the grand opening during this time Sam operated both stores the one in Newport and the one in Benton ville and settled in, quite nicely. They became quite involved with town activities such as Walton served as president of Rotary Club and the Chamber of Commerce. He was elected to the city council and served on the hospital board and in 1954, he started a little l league baseball program on his own. This is only to name a few of this activities and accomplishments in the community. most people would not have time to do anything else but Sam did. He decided to start a second store in Lafayette, located about 20 mile south of Benton ville. This was also named Walton five and dimes but it was not a Ben Franklin Franchise but it was just as successful as the other Walton five and dimes.

Walton knew he needed a qualified manager to run the store so it would be as successful as his other store. Therefore, he said, "I did something I would do for the rest of my run in the retail business without any shame or embarrassment what-so-ever, nose around other people's stores, searching for good talents. With this search, he hired Willard Walker the manger of a variety store in Tulsa. He attracted Walker by offering him a percentage of the store's profits. Now known as profit sharing. Even with this new manager, Sam did not neglect the new store. He visited once a week to make sure everything was running smoothly and once a month he examined the store's books and compiled a profit and loss statement. To keep his stores running in tiptop shape Sam was always trying to find new ideals to improve business.

The next new thing he found was a concept known as self-service. This is that, the cash registers that were located at the counters throughout the store world be replaced by check outs located in the front of the store. Where customers would pay for everything at one time. The cashier would unload the new lightweight baskets, rang the goods up, and put them in bags and the customers happy ready to exit the store. Some other ways Sam kept the customers happy were that he would put on special promotions, kept the place well lighted and clean, demanded that the staff be loyal and did this by sharing a percentage of the profits with the employees. As time passed Sam opened more stores with the help of his brother, father-in-law and brother-in-law. In 1954, he opened a store with his brother in Ruskin Heights a suburb near Kansas City in a shopping center. This store was quite profitable too. He decided to take this ideal to Arkansas but it was not quite as successful as his other stores. At that time Sam decided to go back and just concentrate o n retail business instead of shopping center business. Sam opened a larger stores, which were called Walton's family center. To keep management on their toes and on top of the game Sam offered them the opportunity to become limited partners if they would invest in the store they were to overseen and then invest a maximum of $1000.00 in new outlets as they opened. This kept the managers always trying to keep profits at a maximum.

LES BROWN

As a renowned public speaker, author and television personality, Les Brown has risen to national prominence by delivering a high energy message which tell people how to shake off mediocrity and live up to their greatness. It is a message Les Brown has learned from his own life and one he is helping others apply to their lives.

Born a twin in low-income liberty city in Miami, Florida, Les and his twin brother Wes, were adopted when they were six weeks old, by Mrs. Mamie Brown, a single woman who had very little education and financial means, but a very big heart. As a child his inattention to school work, his restless energy and the failure of his teachers to recognized his real potential resulted in him being mislabeled as a slow learner. The label and the stigma stayed with Les damaging his self-esteem to such an extent that it took several years to o overcome. Les Brown has had no formal education past high school, but with persistence and determination he has initiated and continued a process of unending self-education which has distinguished him an authority on human potential Les Brown's passion to learn and his hunger to realize greatness in himself and others helped him to achieve greatness. He rose from a hip-talking morning Dee-Jay to broadcast manager from community activist to community leader from political commentator to three-term s legislator and from a banquet and nightclub emcee to premier keynote speaker.

In 1986, Les Brown entered the public speaking arena on a full-time basis and formed his own company. Les Brown unlimited Inc. the company provides motivational tapes and materials workshops and personal/ professional development programs aimed at individuals, companies and organizations. In 1989, Les Brown was the recipient of the national speakers association's highest honor. The council of peers Award of Excellence. In addition he was selected to one of America's top five speakers for 1992 by Toastmasters International. In 1990, Les Brown recorded his first series of speech presentation for the public broadcasting system. In 1991, the program entitles "You Deserve With Les Brown", was awarded a Chicago-area Emmy and became the leading fund raising program of it kind for pledges to PBS station nationwide.

Les Brown is not only an internationally recognized speaker and CEO of Les Brown Unlimited, Inc. he is also the author of the highly acclaimed and successful book "Live Your Dreams", and former host of "The Les Brown Show", a nationally syndicated daily television talk show which focused on solutions rather than problems.

Les Brown is one of the nation's leading authorities in understanding and stimulating human potential, utilizing powerful deliverance and newly emerging insights to teach inspire and channel people to new level of achievements.

EARL NIGHTINGALE

As a depression-era child, Earl Nightingale was hungry for knowledge. From the time he as a young boy, he would frequent the long beach public library in California, searching for the answer to the question, "how can a person, starting from scratch, who has no particular advantage in the world, reach the goals that he feels are important to him and by so doing, make a major contribution to o others? His desire to find an answer, coupled with his natural curiosity about the world and its workings spurned him to become one of the world's foremost experts on success and what makes people successful. Earl Nightingale's early career began when, as a member of the Marine Corps, he volunteered to work at a local radio station as an announcer. The marines also gave him a chance to travel, although he only got as far as Hawaii when the Japanese attacked Pearl Harbor in

1941. Earl managed to be one of the few survivors aboard the battleship Arizona.

After five more years in the service, Earl and his wife moved first to Phoenix then Chicago to build what was to be a very fruitful career in network radio. As the host of his own daily commentary program on WGN Earl Nightingale arranged a deal that also gave him a commission on his own advertising sales, by 1957, he was so successful he decided to retire at the age of 35. in the meantime, Earl had bought his own insurance company and had spent many hours motivating its sales force to greater accomplishments when he decided to go on a vacation for an extended period of time, his sales manager begged him to put his inspirational words on record. The result later became the recording entitling "The Strangest Secret".

The first spoken word message to win a gold record by selling over a million copies. In the Strangest Secret, Earl had found an answer to the question that had inspired him as a youth and, in turn, found a way to leave a lasting legacy for others. About this time Earl met a successful businessman by the name of Lioyd Conant and together they began an "Electronic Publishing Company which eventually grew to become a multi—million dollar giant in the Self—Improvement Field. They also developed a syndicated, five minutes daily radio program, Our Changing World, which became the longest – running, most widely syndicated show in radio. When Earl Nightingale died on March 28, 1989, Paul Harvey broke the news to the country on his radio program with the words, "The sonorous voice of the Nightingale was stilled". In the words of his good friend and commercial announcer, Steve King, "Earl Nightingale, never let a day go by that he didn't learn something new and, in turn, pass it on to others, it was his consuming passion".

TONY ROBBINS

Anthony Robbins was born in California on leap year day, February 29, 1960. he became increasingly dissatisfied with the path his life was taking and decided to change it for better. Tony Robbins serves as advisory to some of our country's most influential leaders and has a large number of dedicated followers who don't mind paying thousand of dollars at a time to hear him speak. Tony is a infomercial personality, best known for his motivational courses. He has dedicated the last 25 years of his life to motivating others aside from creating books and courses, he is also known for his charity work. The Anthony Robbins foundation started by handing out bags of groceries anonymously to the underprivileged and has now grown into a organization that feeds 500.000 people worldwide during the holiday seasons.

RIP DANIELS

Since I moved down here in South Mississippi, I have has the pleasure to listen to this man every day on the radio. When I first heard him I was impressed then and still am to this day. I consider him one of my down home heroes. He is the owner of JZ94.5 radio station broadcasting in the Gulfport and Biloxi Mississippi area. Mr Danials is on the air everyday hosting his own radio talk show. He also own Daniels Real Estate Company. This man give a voice to Black Mississippian who have no voice. He's a sounding board to those who have something to say but who are afraid to say it. Most often they find themselves intimidated by others who still think that a good black man is nothing but a black boy that laugh when there's nothing to laugh at, scratch when his body not itching, keep his eyes down on the ground and keep his mouth closed. Mr Daniels story is one of many blacks who started on a journey but for some reason or others took a different road when he came upon that fork in the road. That decision that he made have helped millions, who hear his voice everyday.

Mr Earnest McBride a contributing writer for the Jackson advocate once wrote that Mr Daniels say "that his great—great grandfather fought in the civil war at Vicksburg. Not only is the Mississippi flag historically inaccurate, but it's also an insult to the 200.000 African American Soldiers who fought against it and were victorious. For their descendants to be forced to acknowledge and salute that same flag is a cruel twist of history. It will never be my flag. I don't care what somebody put in their own yard, it might be good for me so I can know who my enemies are. But it can never represent me. And that's the arrogance in the flag vote of two years ago. There's nothing there but sheer arrogance born out of ignorance. The result has been the same as if the flag that those who were fighting against

African American freedom has been successful in the war." This statement is a profound one for it author spoke not as one but he put in words what millions of blacks think when they see that rebel flag flying high in the sky, in someone yard, on their clothes and on their vehicles. I listen to his radio talk show every morning. There are many things that I disagree with him, but also many things I agree with him also. I am inspire by his commitment to excellent. Every day he talk about issues that's inspiring not just to blacks but all people. Anybody who tried to help by informing the little guy on the important issued of the day and tell him or her how they can help themselves to become self empowerment is an asset to his people and his country.

GOALS

GOALS: are predetermined tasks by individuals wired for success in accomplishing a mission. In order to accomplish the mission, goals are the fuel for this achievement. Goals are clear and precise, they are the road map to a successful destination. Ability to set goals and accomplish them are the master key to success. Without them you are simply drifting blindly through life. Goals separate successful people from unsuccessful people. Earl nightingale said that goal is the progressive realization of a worthy ideal. In life we all have twenty four hours. Most unsuccessful people will tell you that they don't have enough time to do anything.

The reason this is truth for them is because when they are at work their mind is back on their family and when they're with their family they're mind is back at work. They spend so much time between wondering if their should be at work or home with the family until their productivity is reduced to nothing more than a wondering generality. Our heavenly father gave each of us a gift. But in order to service him by serving mankind with our gift, we must know :

1. **w**hat the gift is
2. how to developed the gift
3. how to serve the gift to man.

Since goals are your road map, use them to get from where you are now, to where you want to go.

Why are goals important?

Goals are important because they confirm that you are serious about what you are trying to accomplish in life. Without a goals is like facing a thousand roads, "if you don't know where you are going, any road will take you there". One of the main characteristic of successful people are they set goals which are intensely oriented, they know what they want and they are focused single mindlessly on achieving them every single day. I once heard that if you took a stock clerk with goal, you're looking at a future manager or CEO, take a man without goals; well , you're looking at a stock clerk. If you want to increase your confidence, and boost your level of motivation, set for yourself a clear goal. The man or woman with clear and precise goals will cause the universal to open up and embrace them with unforeseen and unlimited opportunities. Goals give you a sense of direction, they add meaning and purpose to your life. Your self-image become stronger, more energized and effective. Your out look on life become one of happiness and profitable.

Why people don't set goals?

There are many reasons why people don't set goals. Mostly they have no ideal of how important they are to the fulfillment in their lives. If you came from a background where no valued was placed on goals or if you socialized with friends of family members that didn't see the significant of goals setting in their lives; nine times out of ten, you want either.

What you need to know about goals.

I want you to know that there is a different between goals and dreams. Both are equally important, but if you really want to become successful then you want to thrive toward your goals for they causes you to take action as the list below dictates.

1. Goals are seriously, clear and precise.
2. They can be both short term and long term.
3. They have a definite time limited.
4. Goals spell out who or what other persons are needed for their obtainment.

5. Goals spell out how they are going to benefit the person involved.
6. To be most effective, goals are written down. They are placed where the originator can read them three or more times a day.
7. Goals become imbedded in the originator mind.

Dreams are not:

1. written down
2. they are not clear or specific
3. mostly they're just wishes
4. they are immeasurable
5. they're just fantasies.

Happiness

It been said that true happiness can only be achieved when people find a sense of meaning and purpose in his or her life. When you wake up in the morning with a purpose, you will find yourself motivated, energized for that day activity. At the end of the day, once you have achieved your objective you will feel a sense of accomplishment, thereby making you more effective and efficiency person. This will increase your confident in yourself. You will begin to believe in you, and once you start on this journey, you're be hard press not to stop. You will push your self to reach and achieve even bigger goals for yourself. Human being are more happy when they control the direction or changes in their life.

Light a match

When you know exactly what you want, light that match and let it become a burning desire in your mind. If this goal become intense enough you will developed the motivation to overcome any obstacles that tried to stand in your way. Be very careful in what you want and ask for in life. Because anything you want bad and long enough you will achieve it. To attain your goals, what sacrifices are you willing to make? What price will you pay? In order to attain your goals, you must make the necessary sacrifice and pay the price first. This is not non negotiable, this is not the type of restaurant where you sit down and eat first then pay for the meal. So think long and hard about your goals, I can't stretch this enough. Don't be like a dog chasing his tail, only to find out later on, it not what he want. You need to know exactly what it is that you are chasing. I will say this over and over time and time again. Ten millions times want be enough. Your goals needs to be crystal clear. If for some reason they are clouded, confusing and you can't find any clarity, I want you to do the following:

A. Check to ensure that what you say you want is what you really want.

At this stage don't concern your self with other people. I know this may sound a little selfish right now. But your goals are your goals. You can't allow someone else to choose them for you. You will never be effective if you do. Your goals must be personal, if they are to have a profound meaning in your life. What concerns are the most important to you right this minute? Do you have financial, business or health concerns? Which of the three are the most important or are they equally important? Choose the one that you would like to work on first.

B. What if money was no object?

If you were rich and struck with nothing but time on your hand and have the objection to choose any professions, do any work or start any business, and you had to work it yourself without getting paid; which would you choose? This is out you determined your true mission or worth in life. Once you have determined what you value the most, there lied your true goal. What if you had a limited time to live and you knew how much of that time you had left, what would you do? What would you strive to complete before leaving this blessed earth? Would you want to travel to some far away land or would you spend more time with the family?

C. What obstacles holding you back?

Are you allowing situation, circumstances, procedures or people get in the way of your success? Why trying to better your life, are you letting pass failures, setbacks and other roadblocks stand in your way? If you are, please ask yourself why? Take a look at any successful person and nine times out of ten, you're find that the individual have fail many times before. It's the pick themselves up attitude and trying again and again that made them what they are today. Remember when I spoke early on making sacrifices and paying the price for your success first before you receive it. Failures are one of the prices you will pay in order to succeed. Failure is not meant to stop you, it just there to make sure you're strong and knowledge enough to make it to the finish line.

If you were making chairs and you could choose from a thousand tree all banded together or you could choose from a hundred trees each separated from each other, and you were concerned with having the most flexible and long lasting chairs; from which trees would you take your pick? Would you choose from the thousand that all banded together or would you choose from the hundred each separated by themselves? I hope that you would choose from the hundred standing all along against the element of nature. For they have bended in all direction that the winds threw at them and time and time again they bended but they did not break nor did they have their brothers to lean on. Because of what they endured, they are more stronger and flexible.

D. Make friend with education

Education is another sacrifice or price you must be willing to make in order to become successful. I believe that education should be a on – going venture in your life anyway. What ever your dream are , you should set out to learn as much as possible about them. The more you know concerning them the greater your success for fulfilling them. The more you know about your job, businesses or anything else, it make you worthy or more valuable. The education you have place on your subject matter determined the quality of services you are able to offer. The more you learn will decide your commitment to excellence in your chosen field. With everything in life the sacrifices and price you 're willing to pay put you in the average categories or the above average. Another way of explaining this is that your earning in life is in direct proportion to your learning.

REPROGRAM YOUR MIND FOR SUCCESS IN 30 DAYS

There is one major thing that stand out among all others that can be directly and proportionately attributed to your successes or failures—your mindset. None of us are born differently in that we all have the same natural aptitude to be as successful in life and business as we want. The difference is whether you have been conditioned to believe that you are not worthy or capable of acquiring abundance and riches. When it comes to acquiring your dreams, there is no external force that's holding you back. Not your parents, your looks or the economy, it is you and only you. So think about that, and ask yourself why are you holding you back? Right now I want to shall with you the recipe for reprogramming your mind in 30 days.

But the most important thing I would like to stretch upon you is your health and your life. What is your goal or your game plan for staying healthy and alive? Staying healthy and alive is not a give me; you must plan and work at staying healthy and alive. You see no amount of money or other material wealth is of any benefit to you, if you are not healthy or alive to enjoy it. Don't just pay lip services or in this case eye services to these words. Words are just words unless you put them into practical use. I want you to become successful, but all success is not good. Some success can be poison. What I mean is, I don't want you to be so focused on becoming successful that you leave yourself out of the equator. It's OK to think about your goals, dreams and achievements. If you don't have your health at the top of your list, then I want you to re-write that list and at the very top put your health. What are you going to do to take better care of your self?

Every day of your life you need to make certain choices. One of the choices that you need to make is your commitment to better health. As we get older, our body began to break down and all types of changes start to take place. If you just set there and take life as it comes, your body will become stiff and fragile. Unused muscles will grow weaker and diminish. Others will more than likely turn into fats, adding stress and other forms of disorders or diseases. It's difficult to enjoy life if you are always in poor health or in pain. Poor health make you poor spiritually.

Most people do not like to eat their vegetables, drink vegetables or fruits juices. In order to stay healthy, you must give your body what it needs instead of what it wants. The body, for the most part, wants what isn't good for it. The body needs a proper diet, exercise and rest. So, on your list at the top of the page I want you to write this in bold lettering; **MY MINDSET MAINTENANCE PLAN**. I want you to follow this plan for thirty days. If you do, I guarantee that you will feel, look and act differently. Your friends will walk up to you and ask you what on earth or you doing. Under the mindset maintenance plan write **number one** and put down **TAKE CARE OF MY SELF.** Under take care of myself I want you to write down **wake-up time**—this will be the time that you will wake up every morning. After writing down **taking care of your personal hygiene**, I want you to write the word **EAT.** I want you to go out and do some studying and researching and find out what are the best healthy foods you can possible get according to your budget. Get a variety of foods so that you can have some fun with mixing and matching different foods so you want get bored eating the same old food every day.

Under eat I want you to write **EXERCISE.** At a minimum I want you to work on your lower body and then your upper body. You can work on your lower body one day and the upper body the next day. You can work on your abs every day, because those muscles repair themselves within a few hours after you finish exercising them. Also at a minimum I want you to do some form of cardiovascular exercises like: walking, running, running in place, or jumping jacks three times a week. **The most important thing I want you to do before you start to work out is go**

to your doctor and tell him or her what you are planning to do and ask for their recommendation according to your present health. Under exercise I want you to write down **LISTEN TO MOTIVATIONAL CD'S OR DVD'S.** You need to listen to somethings motivational at least one hour everyday. Under listen to motivational Cd's or DVD write down **READ AT LEAST TEN TO TWENTY PAGES OF SOMETHINGS MOTIVATIONAL.**

If you would follow this plan, I guarantee you will be a changed person. The late Earl Nightingale once stated, **"you are what you think about, all of us are self—made, you must do the things today that others want do in order to have the things tomorrow that others won't have".**

I remember one of my favorite motivational speaker Les Brown saying **"there is greatness in you, you have more potential in you than you will ever know".** Under reading at least ten to twenty pages of somethings motivational everyday, I want you to write down in bold lettering these words; **ASK AND IT SHALL BE GIVING UNTO YOU. SEEK AND YOU SHALL FIND. KNOCK AND THE DOOR SHALL BE OPEN UNTO YOU, Matthew 7.7 Luke 11.9-13.** Under this I want you to write again in bold print; **MY GOAL.** This is what you want more than anything else. Whatever your dreams are, put them down on paper. If you don't write them down, they mean nothing.

After you write down your goal or goals, I want you to write down **when you expect to accomplish them.** That's right, I want you to give yourself a definite time frame to when you want this done. While you are thinking about your goals, don't be afraid to aim high. You can still be realistic . Look the problem with goals and dreams is not that people aim too high. No it is that they aim to low and hit. Some of you may be saying that you have no idea what you want to do. All I can tell you for sure, God didn't make any mistakes, he put you here for a reason. He gave all of us a gift, and it's high time that you find out what's your purpose for being here. I believe that my gift is to motivate you to greatness. I want to inspire you to look beyond the mirror. When you write them down, I want you to sign your name to it. I want you to visualize yourself as already achieving them.

You have the ability of **Almighty God** in you. You are special; there isn't anyone just like you. Just remember you will become what you think about. I hope that you think about positive things. For if you think positive, you will get positive result. If you think negative things, then you will get negative results. Write your goal down and see your self reaching it; what ever the mind can conceive the mind can achieve. I want you to read this plan everyday, three or more times a day. What this is doing is reprogramming your mind from the way you are presently thinking. The more you do the things that are on this list, the more you will become a different thinking person. If you think differently you will act differently. I really hate repeating myself, but in this case I don't mind. If I can just reach one person, then I have done my job. Do this for thirty days and watch your life change. The only reason you are reading this book is because you are sick and tired of being average. God did not make you to be average. You are a star, so let your light shine before men, so that they can glorify the Lord within you. You really don't know what and who you are until you step outside of the box. Get out of the forest so you can see the trees. Your brain is an untapped universe. There is so much that it is able to do that if you only knew that you didn't know what you think you know, you wouldn't recognize your own self.

LEADERS AND FOLLOWERS
Are you a leader or a follower?

Some people believe that leaders are born and not made. In reality no one were born a leader, instead they developed their skills over time to where it just come natural for them to:

A. Take actions when others want.

B. Speak up when others want.

C. Take charge when others want.

D. Do in spite of fear.

A leader does all of this without being forced. Where by a follower will stand back and wait until someone else:

A. Take actions.

B. Speak up.

C. Take charge

D. DO.

Then they go along half – heartily with the majority. They are relieved that they are not out front, yet when somethings goes wrong, they are first to shake or nod their head as to say I knew it wouldn't work anyway. I would like to concentrate my attention on leaders.

What's makes a bad leader?

Bad leaders, normally are people who does things for themselves. Some qualities of a bad leaders are:

A. Submissive; a person believing in, and following a stronger leader just out of admiration.

B. Inflexible; this person cannot deviate from their course or idea, its their way or the highway.

C. Apprehensive; this person believe everybody's out to get him or her.

D. Aggressive; this person is against anyone who do not agree with them. Their believes, you either with me or against me.

MOTIVATIONAL QUOTES TO HELP YOU REPROGRAM YOUR MINDS

1. "If you're the smartest person in your group; you need to get another group." **Author Unknown**
2. "If you use your energy fighting the wrong fight—you will lose the battle." **Author Unknown**
3. "Choosing success over failure is your decision." **Author Unknown**
4. "Remember you are in charge of your attitude." **Author Unknown**
5. "The people who get on in this world are the people who get up and look for the circumstances they want and if they can't find them, they make them." **George Bernard Shaw**
6. "Winners focus on their strengths and manage their weaknesses." **Byrd Baggett**
7. "He is a wise man who does not grieve for the things which he has not, but rejoices for the those which he has." **Epictetus**
8. "Here is the test to determine whether your mission on earth is finished; If you're alive, it isn't." **Richard Bach**
9. "I claim to be no more than an average man with less than average ability. I am not a visionary. I have not the shadow of a doubt that any man or woman can achieve what I have, if he or she would make the same effort and cultivate the same hope and faith." **Mahandas Gandhi**
10. "Your vision will come clear only when you look into your heart, who look outside, dreams; who looks inside, awaken." **Carl Yung**
11. "There comes a special moment in everyone's life, a moment for which that person was born, That special opportunity, when seizes it, will fulfill his mission. A mission for which he is uniquely qualified. In that moment, he finds greatness. It is his finest hour." **Winston Churchill**
12. "Follow the trail to your dreams not the path of others expectations." **Byrd Baggett**
13. "When you get closer to your greatness, just one more time, one more step, one more knock, one more push or just one more try appealed to be the hardest." **Cleophus Jackson**

14. "To accomplish great things, we must not only act but also dream; not only plan but also believe." **Anotale France**

15. "You can learn the most about people anywhere on earth by asking the question – What is your dream?" **Aluah Simon**

16. "It take 17 muscles to smile and 43 to frown." **Author Unknown**

17. "Worrying is like sitting in a rocking chair.. its give you something to do, but you end up going no where." **Author Unknown**

18. "No one can make you feel inferior without your consent." **Eleanor Roosevelt**

19. "In order to be big, you have to think big. If you think small, you're going to be small." **Emuril Lagasse**

20. "Watch your thoughts, for they become words."
"Chose your words, for they become actions."
"Understand your actions, for they become your character."
"Develop your character, for it becomes your destiny."

21. "It's not what you get in life. It's what you do with it." **Mike Smith**

22. "It's not what you eat, it's what eating you." **Zig Ziglar**

23. "The man who cannot believe in himself cannot believe in anything else." **Author Unknown**

24. "Happiness is a like perfume which you cannot pour on someone without getting some on yourself." **Ralph Waldo**

25. "We are what we pretend to be." **Kurt Vonnegut**

26. "Real knowledge is to know the extent of ones ignorance." **Confucius**

27. "The strongest man in the world is he who stand along." **Herrik Lbson**

28. "In three words I can sum up everything I've learned about life; it goes on." **Robert Frost**

29. "There are three horses who have never come in-win, place, or even show. There names are coulda, woulda and shoulda." **Author Unknown**

30. "Nobody makes a greater mistake than he who does nothing because he could only do a little." **Edmual Burke**

31. "Life doesn't require that we be the best, only that we try our best." **H. Jackson Brown**

32. "I'm still a small boy inside. I only got old on the outside." **Stan L. Zundel**

33. "He that lacks time to mourn, lacks time to mend." **William Shakespeare**
34. "We are what we repeatedly do. Excellence then, is not an act but a habit." **Aristotle**
35. Your attitude determines your altitude." **Author Unknown**
36. "I started out with nothing. I still have most of it." **Michael Davis**
37. "Being broke is a temporary situation, being poor is a state of mind." **Mike Todd**
38. "Remember: you have the courage to be great." **Author Unknown**
39. "Everything changes when you change." **Jim Rohn**
40. " You have been criticizing yourself for years, and it hasn't worked. Try approving of yourself and see what happens." **Louise L. Hay**
41. "Every achiever I ever met says, my life turned around when I began to believe in me." **Robert Shuller**
42. "My heroes are the ones who survived doing it wrong, who made mistakes, and recover from them." **Bono**
43. "The most important thing is this: to be able at any moment to sacrifice what we are for what we might become." **Charles Du Bos**
44. "I am somebody. I am me. I like being me. And I need nobody to make me somebody." **Louis L. Amour**
45. "Don't let life discourage you; everyone who got where he is had to begin where he was." **Richard Evans**
46. "If you have the courage to begin, you have the courage to succeed." **David Viscott**
47. "You don't have to be great to get started but you have to get started to be great." **Les Brown**
48. "It's not what you accomplish in life that matters, it's what you overcome." **Johnny Miller**
49. "You've got to jump off cliffs all the time, and build your wings on the way down." **Ray Bradbury**
50. "In spite of your fear, do what you have to do." **Chin Ning**
51. "Courage is simply the willingness to be afraid and act anyway." **Robert Anthony**
52. "The scars you acquire by exercising courage will never make you feel inferior." **D. A. Battista**

53. "If one dream should fall and break into a thousand pieces, never be afraid to pick one of those pieces up and begin again." Flovia **Weedn**

54. "Focus on where you want to go not o n what you fear." **Anthony Robbin**

55. "If you run into a wall, don't turn around and give up, figure out how to climb it, go through it, or work around it." **Michael Jordan**

56. "If someones says can't that shows you what you to do." **John Cage**

57. "Always concentrate on how far you h ave come, rather than how far you have left to go." **Author Unknown**

58. "Be ready when opportunity comes . . . Luck is the time when preparation and opportunity meet." **Roy D. Chaphan**

59. "Train your head and hands to do, your head and heart to dare." **Joseph Cotter**

60. "Take a chance, all life is a chance. The man who goes furthest is generally the one who is willing to do and dare." **Dale Carnegie's**

61. "Be the change that you want to see in the world." **Mahatma Gandhi**

62. "Choose the job that you love and you will never have to work a day in your life." **Confucius**

63. "There is no real excellence in all this world which can be separated from right living." **David Jordan**

64. "The Lord works from the inside out. The world works from the outside in. The world would take people out of the slums. Christ takes the slums out of people, and then they take themselves out of the slums. The world would mold men by changing their environment. Christ changes men, who then change their environment. The world would shape human behavior, but Christ can change human nature." **Ezra Benson**

65. "So we fix our eyes not on what is seen, but on what is unseen. For what is seen is temporary, but what is unseen is eternal." **2 Cir. 4:18**

66. "Sometimes all the tools we need to succeed are just sitting there waiting for us to discover them." **Author Unknown**

67. "I look forward to a great future for America, a future in which our country will match its military strength with moral restraint . . . an America that will not be afraid of grace and beauty.. and a world which will be safe not only for democracy and diversity, but also for personal distinction." **John F. Kennedy**

68. "The greater the dreams, the higher the obstacles." **Author Unknown**

69. "We must cease from exploration and the end of all our exploring will be to arrive where we began and to know the place for the first time." **T. S. Eliot**

70. "We love by faith, not by sight." **1 Cor. 5.7**

71. "You can't just wish for success. A wish changes nothing; a decision changes everything." **Author Unknown**

72. "The man who gets ahead does more than is necessary – and keeps on doing it." **Author Unknown**

73. "I know of no more encouraging fact than the unquestionable ability of man to elevate his life by conscious endeavor." **Henry Thoreau**

74. "Almost everyone is an opportunity for someone." **Author Unknown**

75. "You are who you are for a reason. You're part of an intricate plan. You're a precious and perfect unique design, called God's special woman or man." **Russell Kelfer**

76. "The law of compensation can work for you or against you depending upon the way you guide it. It may take many years for punishment to follow transgression or for reward to follow virtue, but the compensation always will find you out. Nature makes sure that any excess is followed by a leveling. Fear gives way to the law o f compensation, and envy and malice also disappear from life when one understands how the law of compensation can lead anyone to great success—because anyone can control the way it works for him." **Ralph Waldo Emerson**

77. "Any path which narrows future possibilities may become a lethal trap. Humans are not threading their way through a maze; they scan a vast horizon filled with unique opportunities. The narrowing viewpoint of the maze should appeal only to creatures with their noses buried in sand." **Frank Herbert**

78. "You may know me. I'm your constant companion. I'm your greatest helper. I'm your heaviest burden. I'll push you onward or drag you down to failure. I'm at your command. Half the tasks you do might as well be turned over to me. I'm able to do them quickly. I'm able to do them the same every time. I'm easily managed, all you've got to do is be firm with me. Show me exactly how you want it done; and after a few lessons I'll do it automatically. I'm the servant of all great men and women; Of course, I'm a servant of the failures as well. I've made all the great individuals who have ever been great. And I've made all the failures, too. I work with the precision of a computer and with the intelligence of a human being. You may run me for profit. You may run me to ruin. It makes no difference to me. Be easy with me and I'll destroy you. Be firm with me and I'll put the world at your feet. Who am I? I'm Habit!" **Author Unknown**

79. "We cannot possibly bring out the best in out children unless we're willing to give the best of ourselves." **Crystal Kuykendall**

80. "Things which matter most, must never be at the mercy of things which matter least." **Goethe**

81. "We are the music makers and we are the dreamers of dreams . . . yet we are the movers and shakers of the world forever, it seems." **Arthus O'Shaughnessy**

82. "You never get a second chance to make a first impression." **Author Unknown**

83. "Most of the things worth knowing aren't taught, they;re caught." **Author Unknown**

84. "The greatest need for leadership is in the dark . . . . it is when system is changing so rapidly.. that old prescriptions and old wisdom can only lead to catastrophe, and leadership is necessary to call people to the very strangeness of the new world that is being born." **Kenneth Boulding**

85. "What lies behind us and what lies before us are tiny matters compared to what lies within us." **Oliver Wendell Holmes**

86. "Accept responsibility for your life, know that it is you who will get you where you want to go, no one else." **Les Brown**

87. "A goal property set is halfway reached." **Zig Ziglar**

88. "Immortality is a long shot, I admit, but somebody has to be first." **Bill Cosby**

89. "A friend is one who has the same enemies as you have." **Abraham Lincoln**

90. "Don't let someone else's opinion of you become your reality." **Les Brown**

91. "A lot of people quit looking for work as soon as they find a job." **Zig Ziglar**

92. "I don't know the key to success, but the key to failure is trying to please everybody." **Bill Cosby**

93. "A house divided against itself cannot stand." **Abraham Lincoln**

94. "The more I love people the more I love me, the more I learn about God the less I know about me." **Cleophus Jackson**

95. "Forgive those who have hurt you." **Les Brown**

96. "Every choice you make has an end result." **Zig Ziglar**

97. "Human being are the only creatures on earth that allow their children to come back home." **Bill Cosby**

98. "Am I not destroying my enemies when I make friends of them?" **Abraham Lincoln**

99. "If you fall, fall on your back, if you can look up you can get up." **Les Brown**

100. "If you treat your wife like a thoroughbred you'll never end up with a nag." **Zig Ziglar**

101. "Gray hair is God's graffiti." **Bill Cosby**

102. "As I would not be a slave, so I would not be a master, this expresses my idea of democracy." **Abraham Lincoln**

103. "Help others achieve their dreams and you will achieve yours." **Les Brown**

104. "If you go looking for a friend, you're going to find they"re very scarce. If you go out to be a friend, you're find them everywhere." **Zig Ziglar**

105. "In order to succeed, your desire for success should be greater than your fear of failure." **Bill Cosby**

106. "Avoid popularity if you would have peace." **Abraham Lincoln**

107. "If you put yourself in a position where you have to stretch outside your comfort zone, then you are forced to expand your consciousness." **Les Brown**

108. "If you can dream it, then you can achieve it. You will get all you want in life if you help enough other people get what they want." **Zig Ziglar**

109. "Like everyone else who makes the mistake of getting older, I begin each day with coffee and obituaries." **Bill Cosby**

110. "Better to remain silent and be thought a fool then to speak out and remove all doubt." **Abraham Lincoln**

111. "I spend sixteen hours everyday finding myself and eight hours forgetting what I found." **Cleophus Jackson**

112. "Life has no limitation, except the ones you make." **Les Brown**

113. "Inspire your mind." **Dr. Wayne Dyer**

114. "It take someone with a vision of the possibilities to attain new levels of experiences. Someone with the courage to live his dreams." **Les Brown**

115. "If you learn form defeat, you haven't really lost." **Zig Ziglar**

116. "Nothing I've ever done has given me more joys and rewards than being a father to my own children." **Bill Cosby**

117. "Books serve to show a man that those original thoughts of his aren't very new at all." **Abraham Lincoln**

118. "Stop acting as if life is a rehearsal. Live this day as if it were your last. The past is over and gone. The future is not guaranteed." **Dr. Wayne Dyer**

119. "Just because fate doesn't deal you the right cards, it doesn't mean you should give up. It just mean you have to play the cards you get the maximum potential." **Les Brown**

120. "It's not what you've got, it's what you use that makes a different." **Zig Ziglar**

121. "There is no way to prosperity, prosperity is the way." **Dr. Wayne Dyer**

122. "Reviews your goals twice everyday in order to be focused on achieving them." **Les Brown**

123. "Many marriage would be better if the husband and the wife clearly understood that they are on the same side." **Zig Ziglar**

124. "Old is always fifteen years from now." **Bill Cosby**

125. "Character is like a tree and reputation like a shadow, the shadow what we think of it; the tree is the real thing." **Abraham Lincoln**

126. "Common looking people are the best in the world; that is the reason the Lord makes so many of them." **Abraham Lincoln**

127. "Everything you are against weakens you. Everything you are for empowers you." **Dr. Wayne Dyer**

128. "Shoot for the moon and if you miss you will still be among the stars." **Les Brown**

129. "Success is dependent upon the glands—sweat glands." **Zig Ziglar**

130. "Give me six hours to chop down a tree and I will spend the first four sharpening the ax." **Abraham Lincoln**

131. "I cannot always control what goes on outside but I can always control what goes on inside." **Dr. Wayne Dyer**

132. "Someone's sitting in the shade today because someone planted a tree a long time ago." **Author Unknown**

133. "The foundation stones for a balanced success are honesty, character, integrity, faith, love and loyalty." **Zig Ziglar**

134. "Everybody likes a compliment." **Abraham Lincoln**

135. "Centered and not focused on harming others, is stronger than any physical force in the universe." **Dr. Wayne Dyer**

136. "The only limits to the possibilities in your life tomorrow are the buts you use today." **Les Brown**

137. "The way you see people is the way you treat them." **Zig Ziglar**

138. "I am not bound to succeed, but I am bound to live by the light that I have. I must stand with anybody that stand right, and stand with him when he is right, and apart with him when he goes wrong." **Abraham Lincoln**

139. "All human actions have one or more of these seven causes; chance, nature, compulsions, habit, reason, passion and desire." **Aristotle**

140. "Be as you wish to be seem." **Socrates**

141. "A good decision is based on knowledge and not on numbers." **Plato**

142. "I live not to become who I am but I become who I am to live." **Cleophus Jackson**

143. "All philosophy live in two words; sustain and abstain." **Epictetus**

144. "A superior man is modest in his speech, but exceeds in his actions." **Confucius**

145. "All paid jobs absorb and degrade the mind." **Aristotle**

146. "By all means, marry if you get a good wife, you"ll become happy if you get a bad one, you"ll become a philosopher." **Socrates**

147. "All the gold which is under or upon the earth is not enough to give in exchange for virtue." **Plato**
148. "All religions must be tolerated – for every man must get to heaven in his own way." **Epictetus**
149. "Ability will never catch up with the demand for it." **Confucius**
150. "Character is long – standing habit." **Plutarch**
151. "Anybody can become angry – that is easy, but to be angry with the right person and to the right degree and at the right time and for the right purpose, and in the right way, that is not within everybody's power and it is not easy." **Aristotle**
152. "A friend to all is a friend to none." **Aristotle**
153. "I shall assume that your silence gives consent." **Plato**
154. "Control thy passions lest they take vengeance on thee." **Epictetus**
155. "And remember, no matter where you go, then you are." **Confucius**
156. "Do not speak of your happiness to one less fortunate than yourself." **Plutarch**
157. "Blushing is the color of virtue." **Diogenes**
158. "A great city is not to be confounded with a populous one." **Aristotle**
159. "If a man neglects education, he walks lame to the end of his life." **Plato**
160. "Money is not the root and stem of all evil but ignorance, is the root and stem of all evil." **Cleophus Jackson**
161. "Do not laugh much or often or unrestrained." **Epictetus**
162. "Choose a job that you love, and you will never have to work a day in your life." **Confucius**
163. "Friendship is essentially a partnership." **Aristotle**
164. "Employ your time is improving yourself by other men writing, so that you shall give easily what others have labored hard for." **Socrates**
165. "I am the wisest man alive, for I know one thing and that is that I know nothing." **Socrates**
166. "If one way be better than another, that you may be sure is nature's way." **Aristotle**
167. "Knowledge becomes evil if the aim be not virtuous." **Plato**

168. "First learn the meaning of what you say, and then speak," **Epictetus**

169. "By three methods we learn wisdom; first by reflection, which is noblest, second by imitation which is easiest and third by experience, which is the bitterest." **Confucius**

170. "I do not need a friend who changes when I change and who nods when I nod, my shadow does that much better." **Plutarch**

171. "If all misfortunes where laid in one common heap whence everyone must take an equal portion, most people would be contented to take their own and depart." **Socrates**

172. "Life must be lived as play." **Play**

173. "First say to yourself what you would be; and then do what you have to do." **Epictetus**

174. "Everything has beauty, but not everyone sees it." **Confucius**

175. "Know how to listen, and you will profit even from those who talk badly." **Aristotle**

176. "Let him that would moved the world first move himself." **Socrates**

177. "He who is not a good servant will not be a good master." **Plato**

178. "God has entrusted me with myself." **Epictetus**

179. "He who learns but does not think is lost; he who think but does not learn is in great danger." **Confucius**

180. "Neither blame or praise yourself." **Plutarch**

181. "He has the most who is most content with the least." **Diogenes**

182. "Education is the best provision for old age." **Aristotle**

183. "Once made equal to man, woman becomes his superior." **Socrates**

184. "Man – a being in search of meaning." **Plato**

185. "He is a drunkard who take more than three glasses though he be not drunk." **Epictetus**

186. "Silence at the proper season is wisdom, and better than any speech." **Plutarch**

187. "I have nothing to ask but that you would remove to the other side, that you may not by intercepting the sunshine, take from me what you cannot give." **Diogenes**

189. "Excellence is an art won by training and habituation, we do not act rightly because we have virtue or excellence but we rather have those because we have acted rightly, we are what we repeatedly do, excellence then is not an act but a habit." **Aristotle**

190. "The end of life is to be likes God, and the soul following God will be like him." **Socrates**

191. "Any man may easily do harm, but not every man can do good to another." **Plato**

192. "Fear is pain arising from the anticipation of evil." **Aristotle**

193. "The greatest way to live with honor in this world is to be what we pretend to be." **Socrates**

194. "He is a wise man who does not grieve for the things which he has not, but rejoices for those which he has." **Epictetus**

195. "I hear and I forget, I see and I remember, I do and I understand." **Confucius**

196. "The mind is not a vessels to be filled but a fire to be kindled." **Plutarch**

197. "He who hath many friends hath none." **Aristotle**

198. "And what, Socrates, is the food of the soul? Surely , I said knowledge is the food of the soul." **Plato**

199. "If evil be spoken of you and it be true, correct yourself, if it be a lie, laugh at it." **Epictetus**

200. "If you think in terms of a year, plant a seed, if in term of ten years, plant trees; if in terms of 100 years, teach the people." **Aristotle**

201. "The omission of good is no less reprehensible then the commission of evil." **Plutarch**

202. "In a democracy the poor will have more power then the rich, because there are more of them, and the will of the majority is supreme." **Epictetus**

203. "No one loves the man whom he fears." **Aristotle**

204. "As the builders say, the larger stones do not lie well without the lesser." **Plato**

205. "If thy brother wrong thee, remember not so much hes wrong doing, but more than ever that he is thy brother." **Epictetus**

206. "It does not matter how slowly you go as long as you do not stop." **Confucius**

207. "Those who aim at great deeds must also suffer greatly." **Plutarch**

208. "I threw my cup away when I saw a child drinking from his hands at the trough." **Diogenes**

209. "Quality is not an act, it is a habit." **Aristotle**

210. "Worthless people live only to eat and drink; people o f worth eat and drink only to live." **Socrates**

211. "At the touch of love everyone becomes a poet." **Plato**

212. "If you want to improve, be content to be thought foolish and stupid." **Epictetus**

213. "Life is really simple, but we insist on making it complicated." **Confucius**

214. "What we achieve inwardly will change outer reality." **Plutarch**

215. "The aim of the wise is not to secure pleasure but to avoid pain." **Aristotle**

216. "Better a little which is well done, than a great deal imperfectly." **Plato**

217. "If you want to be a writer, write." **Epictetus**

218. "The educated differ from the uneducated as much as the living from the dead." **Aristotle**

219. "Nothing in the affairs of men is worthy of great anxiety." **Plato**

220. "Never contract friendship with a man that is not better then thyself." **Confucius**

221. "To find fault is easy; to do better may be difficult." **Plutarch**

222. "The Gods too are fond of a joke." **Aristotle**

223. "Death is not the worst that can happen to men." **Plato**

224. "It is impossible to begin to learn that which one think one already knows." **Epictetus**

225. "No matter how busy you may think you are, you must find time for reading, or surrender yourself to self – chosen ignorance." **Confucius**

226. "The soul never thinks without a picture." **Aristotle**

227. "In making a speech one must study three points; first the means of producing persuasion; second, the language, third the proper arrangement of the various parts of the speech.: **Aristotle**

228. "For a man to conquest himself is the first and noblest of all victories." **Plato**

229. "It takes more than just a good looking body you've got to have the heart and soul to go with it." **Epictetus**

230. "Only the wisest and stupidest of men never change." **Confucius**

231. "To be ignorant of the lives of the most celebrated men of antiquity is to continue in a state of childhood all our days." **Plutarch**

232. "It take a wise man to discover a wise man." **Diogenes**

233. "The God in me teaches me to get to know myself everyday." **Cleophus Jackson**

234. "In nine cases out of ten, a woman had better show more affection then she feel." **Aristotle**

235. "Human behavior flows from three main sources; desire, emotion, and knowledge." **Plato**

236. "It's not what happens to you but how you react to it that matters." **Epictetus**

237. "Silence is a true friend who never betrays." **Confucius**

238. "All men are by nature equal, made all of the same earth by one workman; and however we deceive ourselves as dear unto God is the poor peasant as the mighty prince." **Plato**

239, "Courage is a kind of salvation." **Plato**

240. "No great thing is created suddenly." **Epictetus**

241. "It is the mark of an education mind to be able to entertain a thought without accepting it." **Aristotle**

242. "A fool thinks himself to be wise, but a wise man knows himself to be a fool." **William Shakespeare**

243. "A penny saved is a penny earned." **Benjamin Franklin**

244. "A fanatic is one who can't change his mind and won't change the subject." **Winston Churchill**

245. "Every time my mind is made up; I find something to change it." **Cleophus Jackson**

246. "There is no greater agony than bearing an untold story inside of you." **Maya Angelou**

247. "Be not afraid of greatness; some are born great, some achieve greatness, and some have greatness thrust upon them." **William Shakespeare**

248. "Any society that would give up a little liberty to gain a little security will deserve neither and lose both." **Benjamin Franklin**

249. "We make a living by what we get, but we make a life by what we give." **Winston Churchill**

250. "History, despite its wrenching pain, cannot be unlived; but if forced with courage, need not be lived again." **Maya Angelou**

251. "A bank is a place where they lend you an umbrella in fair weather and ask for it back when it begin to rain." **Robert Frost**

252. "Suppose God is black? What if we go to heaven and we, all our lives have treated the negro as an inferior, and God is there, and we look up and he is not white? What then is our response?" **Robert Kennedy**

253. "All the world's a stage, and all the men and women merely players: they have their exits and their entrances; and one man in his time plays many parts, his act being seven ages." **William Shakespeare**

254. "The use of money is all the advantage there is in having it." **Benjamin Franklin**

255. "A lie gets halfway around the world before the truth has a chance to get its pants on." **Winston Churchill**

256. "I love to see a young girl go out and grab the world by the lapels. Life's a bitch. You've got to go out and kick ass." **Maya Angelou**

257. "A mother takes twenty years to make a man of her boy, and another woman makes a fool of him in twenty minutes." **Robert Frost**

258. "Only those who dare to fail greatly can ever achieve greatly." **Robert Kennedy**

259. "Better three hours too soon than a minute too late." **William Shakespeare**

260. "Eat to please thyself, but dress to please others." **Benjamin Franklin**

261. "A pessimist sees the difficulty in every opportunity, an optimist sees the opportunity in every difficulty." **Winston Churchill**

262. "I've learned that you shouldn't go through life with a catcher mitt on both hands; you need to be able to throw something back." **Maya Angelou**

263. "Don't ever take a fence down until you know why it was put up." **Robert Frost**

264. "There are those who look at things the way they are, and ask why— I dream of things that never were, and ask why not?" **Robert Kennedy**

265. "What's in a name? That which we call a rose by any other name would smell as sweet." **William Shakespeare**

266. "Energy and persistence conquer all things." **Benjamin Franklin**

267. "If you're going through hell, keep going." **Winston Churchill**

268. "People will forget what you said, people will forget what you did, but people will never forget how you made them feel." **Maya Angelou**

269. "Tragedy is a tool for the living to gain wisdom, not a guide by which to live." **Robert Kennedy**

270. "If freedom of speech is taken away then dumb and silent we may be led, like sheep to the slaughter." **George Washington**

271. "And oftentimes excusing of a fault doth make the fault the worse by the excuse." **William Shakespeare**

272. "Never, never, never give up." **Winston Churchill**

273. "If you don't like something, change it, if you can't change it, change your attitude." **Maya Angelou**

274. "Forgive me my nonsense, as I also forgive the nonsense of those that think they talk sense." **Benjamin Franklin**

275. "Associate with men of good quality if you esteem your own reputation, for it better to be alone then in bad company." **George Washington**

276. "Love all, trust a few, do wrong to none." **William Shakespeare**

277. "Tell me and I forget. Teach me and I remembered. Involve me and I learn." **Benjamin Franklin**

278. "A man does what he must, in spite of personal consequences, in spite o f obstacles and dangers and pressures—and that is the basis of all human morality." **Winston Churchill**

279. "Love recognizes no barriers. It jumps hurdles, leap fences, penetrates walls to arrive at it destination full of hope." **Maya Angelou**

280. "Half the world is composed of people who have something to say and can't, and the other half who have nothing to say and keep on saying it." **Robert Frost**

281. "Stop telling me what I can't do, if you really care, lend me a hand." **Cleophus Jackson**
282. "Our doubts are traitors and makes us lose the good we often might win, by fearing to attempt." **William Shakespeare**
283. "Either write something worth reading or do something worth writing." **Benjamin Franklin**
284. "All the great things are simple, and many can be expressed in a single word; freedom, justice, honor, duty, mercy and hope." **Winston Churchill**
285. "Nothing will work unless you do." **Maya Angelou**
286. "I am a writer of books in retrospect. I talk in order to understand. I teach in order to learn." **Robert Frost**
287. "In order to be right I need to wrong you then my righteousness lose it's meaning." **Cleophus Jackson**
288. "There is nothing either good or bad but thinking makes it so." **William Shakespeare**
289. "Courage is what it takes to stand up and speak; courage is also what it takes to sit down and listen." **Winston Churchill**
290. "While I know myself as a creation of God, I am also obligated to realize and remember that every one else and everything else are also God's creation." **Maya Angelou**
291. "Seek freedom and become captive of your desires, seek discipline and find your liberty." **Frank Herbert**
292. "Insanity is doing the same thing, over and over again, and expecting different results." **Albert Einstein**
293. "Art is a beautiful way of doing things, science is the effective way of doing things, business is the economical way of doing things." **Elbert Hubbard**
294. "Success is to be measured not so much by the position that one has reached in life as by the obstacles which he has overcome." **Booker T. Washington**
295. "It does not take much strength to do things, but it requires great strength to decide on what to do." **Elbert Hubbard**
296. "Without change, something sleeps inside us, and seldom awakens, the sleeper must awaken." **Frank Herbert**
297. "The difference between stupidity and genius is that genius has its limits." **Albert Einstein**

298. "We must reinforce argument with results." **Booker T. Washington**

299. "The question isn't at what age I want to retire, it's at what income." **George Foreman**

300. "So you hate life; tell me what have life giving you that you didn't give life? " **Cleophus Jackson**

301. "Initiative is doing the right things without being told." **Elbert Hubbard**

302. "Any road followed precisely to its end leads precisely nowhere. Climb the mountain just to test it's a mountain." **Frank Herbert**

303. "One man cannot hold another man down in the ditch without remaining down in the ditch with him." **Booker T. Washington**

304. "A man who read too much, and used his own brain too little falls into lazy habits of thinking." **Albert Einstein**

305. "In order to have friends, you must first be one." **Elbert Hubbard**

306. "Everybody wants to be somebody. The thing you have to do is give them confidence, you have to give a kid a dream." **George Foreman**

307. "I let no man drag me down so low as to make me hate him." **Booker T. Washington**

308. "To suspect your own mortality is to know the beginning of terror, to learn irrefutably that you are mortal is to know the end of terror." **Frank Herbert**

309. "If you can't explain it simply, you don't understand it well enough." **Albert Einstein**

310. "If you suffer, thank God, it is a sure sign that you are alive." **Elbert Hubbard**

311. "If you can't read, it's going to be hard to realize dreams." **Booker T. Washington**

312. "Mystery to myself, who am I ? the mirror says back, the George you was always meant to be. It wasn't always like that, used to look in the mirror and cried a river." **George Foreman**

313. "Education is what remains after one has forgotten what one has learned in school." **Albert Einstein**

314. "If you think of yourselves as helpless and ineffectual, it certain that you will create a despotic government to be your master." **Frank Herbert**

315. "If you want to lift yourself up, lift up someone else." **Booker T. Washington**

316. "If pleasures are greatest in anticipation, just remember that this is also true of trouble." **Elbert Hubbard**

317. "An attempt to combine wisdom and powers has only rarely been successful and then only for a short while." **Albert Einstein**

318. "I would rather be able to appreciate things I cannot have than to have things I am not able to appreciate." **Elbert Hubbard**

319. "This is my gift, I let negativity roll off me like water off a duck's back. If it not positive, I didn't hear it. If you can overcome that, fights are easy." **George Foreman**

320. "Think you of the fact that a deaf person cannot hear. Than what deafness may we not all possess? What senses do we lack that we cannot see and cannot hear? What world all around us we do not know?" **Frank Herbert**

321. "There are two ways of exerting one's strength' one is pushing down, the other is pulling up." **Booker T. Washington**

322. "If we knew what we were doing, it would not be called research, would it?" **Albert Einstein**

323. "How many a man has throwing up his hands, at a time when a little more effort, a little more patience would have achieved success." **Elbert Hubbard**

324. "Put your name on something, it better be the best; you only get one shot." **George Foreman**

325. "No greater injury can be done to any youth then to let him feel that because he belong to this or that race he will be advanced in life regardless of his own merits or efforts." **Booker T. Washington**

326. "Wealth is a tool of freedom, but the pursuit of wealth is the way to slavery." **Frank Herbert**

327. "Great spirits have always encountered violent opposition from mediocre minds." **Albert Einstein**

328. "He who does not understand your silence will probably not understand your words." **Albert Einstein**

329. "The individual who can do something that the world wants done will, in the end, make his way regardless of his race." **Booker T. Washington**

330. "Anyone who doesn't take truth seriously in small matter cannot be trusted in large one either." **Albert Einstein**

331. "Dignify and glorify common labor, it is at the bottom of life that we must begin, not at the top." **Booker T. Washington**

332. "The difference between sentiment and being sentimental is the following: sentiment is when a driver swerves out of the way to avoid hitting a rabbit on the road. Being sentimental is when the same driver when swerving away from the rabbit hits a pedestrian." **Frank Herbert**

333. "We cannot solve our problems with the same thinking we used when we created them." **Albert Einstein**

334. "I write often to think, the more I write the better I think." **Cleophus Jackson**

335. "He has achieved success who has worked well, laughed often and loved much." **Elbert Hubbard**

336. "Nothing even come to one, that is worth having except as a result of hard work." **Booker T. Washington**

337. "The secret to creativity is knowing how to hide your sources." **Albert Einstein**

338. "To attempt seeing truth without knowing falsehood it is the attempt to see the light without knowing the dark, it cannot be." **Frank Herbert**

339. "Friendship, like credit, is highest when it is not used." **Elbert Hubbard**

340. "No man, who continues to add something to the material, intellectual and moral well being of the place in which he lives, is left long without proper reward." **Booker T. Washington**

341. "Be nice to nerds. Chances are you'll end up working for one." **Bill Gates**

342. "You don't have to be the biggest to beat the biggest." **Ross Perot**

343. "If you come to fame not understanding who you are, it will define who you are." **Oprah Winfrey**

344. "A great attitude does much more than turn on the lights in our worlds, it seems to magically connect us to all sorts of serendipitous opportunities that were somehow absent before the change." **Earl Nightingale**

345. "If I'd had some idea of a finish line, don't you think I would have crossed it years ago?" **Bill Gates**

346. "Inventories can be managed, but people must be led." **Ross Perot**

347. "Lots of people want to ride with you in the limo, but what you really want to know; who will take the bus with you when the limo break down ." **Oprah Winfrey**

348. "All you have to do is know where you're going. The answer will come to you of their own accord." **Earl Nightingale**

349. "I believe that if you show people the problems and you show them the solutions they will be move to act." **Bill Gates**

350. "Most people give up just when they're about to achieve success they quit on the one yard line. They give up at the last minute of the game one foot from a winning touchdown." **Ross Perot**

351. "I am a woman in process. I'm just trying like everybody else. I try to take every conflict, every experiences, and learn from it." **Oprah Winfrey**

352. "All you need is the plan, this road map, and the courage to press on to your destination." **Earl Nightingale**

353. "If you can't make it good, at least make it look good." **Bill Gates**

354. "Eagles don't flock. You have to find them one at a time." **Ross Perot**

355. "Breathe, let go, and remind yourself that this very moment is the only one you know you have for sure." **Oprah Winfrey**

356. "Any people who contributes to prosperity must profit in turn." **Earl Nightingale**

357. "If you think your teacher is tough, wait until you get a boss, he doesn't have tenure." **Bill Gates**

358. "If you see a snake, just kill it, don't appoint a committee on snake." **Ross Perot**

359. "I don't think of myself as a poor deprived ghetto girl who make good. I think of myself as somebody who from an early age knew I was responsible for myself, and I had to make good." **Oprah Winfrey**

360. "Creativity is a natural extension of out enthusiasms." **Earl Nightingale**

361. "In this business, by the time you realize you're in trouble, it's too late to save yourself. Unless you're running scared all the time you're gone." **Bill Gates**

362. "If someone is blessed as I am is not willing to clean out the barn, who will?" **Ross Perot**

363. "Doing the best at this moment puts you in the best place for the next moment." **Oprah Winfrey**

364. "Our attitude towards others determines their attitude toward us." **Earl Nightingale**

365. "Intellectual property has the shelf life of a banana." **Bill Gates**

366. "Business is not just doing deals; business in having great products, doing great engineering, and providing tremendous service to customers, finally; business is a cobweb of human relationships." **Ross Perot**

367. "Turn your wounds into wisdom." **Oprah Winfrey**

368. "Our environment, the world in which we live and work, is a mirror of our attitude and expectations." **Earl Nightingale**

369. "It's fine to celebrate success but it is more important to heed the lessons of failure." **Bill Gates**

370. "In plain Texas talk, it's do the right things." **Ross Perot**

371. "Where there is no struggle, there is no strength." **Oprah Winfrey**

372. "Learn to enjoy every minute of your life, be happy now, don"t wait for something outside of yourself to make you happy in the future." **Earl Nightingale**

373. "Life is not divided into semesters. You don't get summers off and very few employers are interested in keeping you from yourself." **Bill Gates**

374. "The activist is not the man who says the river is dirty. The activist is the man who cleans up the river." **Ross Perot**

375. "People are where they are because that is exactly where they really want to be, whether they will admit that or not." **Earl Nightingale**

376. "People always fear change , people feared electricity when it was invented, didn't they? People feared coal, they feared gas powered engines. There will always be ignorance, and ignorance lead to fear. But with time, people will come to accept their silicon master." **Bill Gates**

377. "War has rules, mud wrestling has rules, politic has no rules." **Ross Perot**

378. "Ideas are elusive, slippery things. Best to keep a pad of paper and a pencil at your bedside, so you can stab them during the night before they get away." **Earl Nightingale**

379. "Always keep that attitude, pretend that you are holding a beautiful fragrant bouquet." **Earl Nightingale**

380. "Executive ability is deciding quickly and getting somebody else to do the work." **Earl Nightingale**

381. "Get into a line that you will find to be a deep personal interest, something you really enjoy spending twelve to fifteen hours a day working at, and the rest of the time thinking about." **Earl Nightingale**

382. "Don't let the fear of the time it will take to accomplish something stand in the way of your doing it, the time will pass anyway. We might just as well put that passing time to the best possible use." **Earl Nightingale**

383. "Picture yourself in your minds eye as having already achieved the goal, see yourself doing the things you'll be doing when you've reached your goal." **Earl Nightingale**

384. "People with goals succeed because they know where they're going." **Earl Nightingale**

385. "Everything in the world we want to do or get done, we must do with and through people." **Earl Nightingale**

386. "The mind moves in the direction of our currently dominant thoughts." **Earl Nightingale**

387. "We will receive not what we idly wish for but what we justly earn, our rewards will always be in exact proportion to our services." **Earl Nightingale**

388. "Your world is a living expression of how you are using and have used your mind." **Earl Nightingale**

389. "The big thing is that you know what you want." **Earl Nightingale**

390. "What ever we plant in out subconscious mind and nourish with repetition and emotion will one day become a reality." **Earl Nightingale**

391. "You can measure opportunity with the some yardstick that measures the risk involved, they go together." **Earl Nightingale**

392. "The biggest mistake that you can make is to believe that you are working for somebody else, job security is gone." **Earl Nightingale**

393. "You are at this moment, standing, right in the middle of your own acres of diamonds." **Eight Nightingale**

394. "When ever we're afraid, it's because we don't know enough, if we understood enough, we would never be afraid." **Earl Nightingale**

395. "Excellence always sells." **Earl Nightingale**

396. "I pray to die at an old age with a young man body and soul; even then, I will my ghost to inspire and motivate others." **Cleophus Jackson**

397. "A goal is a dream with a deadline." **Napoleon Hill**

398. "Action is the real measure of intelligence." **Napoleon Hill**

399. "All achievements, all earned riches, have their beginning in an idea." **Napoleon Hill**

400. "All the breaks you need in life wait within your imagination. Imagination is the workshop of your mind, capable of turning mind energy into accomplishment and wealth." **Napoleon Hill**

401. "Any idea, plan, or purpose maybe placed in the mind through repetition of thought." **Napoleon Hill**

402. "Before success comes, in any man's life, he's sure to meet with much temporary defeat and perhaps some failures. When defeat overtakes a man, the easiest and the most logical thing to do is to quit, that's exactly when the majority of men do." **Napoleon Hill**

403. "Big pay and little responsibility are circumstances seldom found together." **Napoleon Hill**

404. "Cherish your visions and your dreams as they are the children of your soul, the blueprint o f your ultimate achievements." **Napoleon Hill**

405. "Create a definite plan for carrying out your desire and begin at once, whether you ready or not, to put this plan into action." **Napoleon Hill**

406. "Don't wait, the time will never be just right." **Napoleon Hill**

407. "Edison failed 10, 000 times before he made the electric light. Do not be discouraged if you fail a few times." **Napoleon Hill**

408. "Education comes from within, you get it by struggle and effort and thought." **Napoleon Hill**

409. "Effort only fully releases its rewards after a person refuses to quit." **Napoleon Hill**

410. "Every adversity, every failure, every heart ache carries with it the seed of an equal or greater benefit." **Napoleon Hill**

411. "Every person who win in any undertaking must be willing to cut all sources of retreat. Only by doing so can one be sure of maintaining that state of mind know as a burning desire to win, essential to success." **Napoleon Hill**

412. "Great achievement is usually born of great sacrifice, and is never the result of selfishness." **Napoleon Hill**

413. "Hold a picture of yourself long and steadily enough is your mind's eye, and you will be drawn toward it." **Napoleon Hill**

414. "If you cannot do great things, do small things in a great way." **Napoleon Hill**

415. "If you do not conquer self, you will be conquered by self." **Napoleon Hill**

416. "If you must speak ill of another, do not speak it, write it in the sand near the water's edge." **Napoleon Hill**

417. "It is always your next move." **Napoleon Hill**

418. "It takes half your life before you discover life is a do it yourself project." **Napoleon Hill**

419. "Just as our eyes need light in order to see, our mind need ideas in order to conceive." **Napoleon Hill**

420. Money without brains is always dangerous." **Napoleon Hill**

421. "More gold has been mined from the thoughts of men, then has been taking from the earth." **Napoleon Hill**

422. "Nature cannot be tricked or cheated, she will give you up to you the object of your struggles , only after you have paid her price." **Napoleon Hill**

423. "No man can succeed in a line of endeavor which he does not like." **Napoleon hill**

424. "No man ever achieved worth while success who did not at one time or other, find himself with at least one foot hanging well over the brink of failure." **Napoleon Hill**

425. "No man is ever whipped until he quit in his own mind." **Napoleon Hill**

426. "Opportunity often comes disguised in the form of misfortune or temporary defeat." **Napoleon Hill**

427. "Patience, persistence and perspiration make an unbeatable combination for success." **Napoleon Hill**

428. "The ladder of success is never crowded at the top. **Napoleon Hill**

429. "The man who does more than he is paid for will soon be paid for more then he does." **Napoleon Hill**

430. "Even a mistake may turn out to be the one thing necessary to a worth while achievement." **Henry Ford**

431. "I am looking for a lot of men who have an infinite capacity to not know what can't be done." **Henry Ford**

432. "If you think you can do a thing or think you can't do a thing, you're right." **Henry Ford**

433. "Nothing is particularly hard if you divide it into small jobs." **Henry Ford**

434. "Coming together is a beginning, keeping together is progress, working together is success." **Henry Ford**

435. "You can't build a reputation on what you are going to do." **Henry Ford**

436. "My best friend is the one who bring out the best in me." **Henry Ford**

437. "An idealist is a person who help other people to be prosperous." **Henry Ford**

438. "Anyone who stops learning is old, whether at twenty or eighty. Anyone who keeps learning stays young. The greatest thing in life is to keep your mind young." **Henry Ford**

439. "You will find men who want to be carried on the shoulders of others, who think that the world owes them a living. They don't seem to see that we must all lift together and pull together." **Henry Ford**

440. "You can't learn in school what the world is going to do next year." **Henry Ford**

441. "It is not the employer who pays the wages. Employers only handle the money. It is the customers who pays the wages." **Henry Ford**

442. "Money is like an arm or leg, use it or lose it." **Henry Ford**

443. "Thinking is the hardest work there is, which is probably the reason why so few engage in it." **Henry Ford**

444. "Most people spend more time and energy going around problems than in trying to solve them." **Henry Ford**

445. "What's right about America is that although we have a mess of problems, we have great capacity intellect and resources to do something about them." **Henry Ford**

446. "The competitor to be feared is one who never bothers about you at all, but goes on making his own business better all the time." **Henry Ford**

447. "There is joy in work, there is no happiness except in the realization that we have accomplished something." **Henry Ford**

448. "There is one rule for industrialist and that is make the best quality of goods possible at the lowest cost possible, paying the highest wages possible." **Henry Ford**

449. "There is no man living that cannot do more than he think." **Henry Ford**

450. "The only real security that a man can have in this world is a reserve of knowledge, experiences and ability." **Henry Ford**

451. "As we advance in life we learn the limits of our abilities." **Henry Ford**

452. "Before anything else, getting ready is the secret of success." **Henry Ford**

453. "I believe God is managing affairs and that he doesn't need any advice from me. With God in charge I believe everything will work out for the best, in the end. So what is there to worry about?" **Henry Ford**

454. "Don't find fault, find a remedy." **Henry Ford**

455. "When one door closes another door opens; but we often look so long and so regretfully, upon the closed door that we do not see the ones which open for us." **Alexander Graham Bell**

456. "How far you go in life depends on your being tender with the young, compassionate with the aged, sympathetic with the striving and tolerant of the weak and strong. Because someday in your life you will have been all of these." **George Washington Carver**

457. "Anything will give up its secrets if you love it enough. Not only have I found that when I talk to the little flowers or to the little

peanut they will give up their secrets, but I have found that when I silently commune with people they give up their secrets also, if you love them enough." **George Washington Carver**

458. "As a well spent day bring happy sleep, so life well used brings happy death." **Leonardo DA Vinci**

459. "Just because something doesn't do what you planned it to do doesn't mean it's useless." **Thomas A. Edison**

460. "Many of life's failures are people who did not realize how close they were to success when they gave up." **Thomas A. Edison**

461. "There is no expedient to which a man will not go to avoid the labor of thinking." **Thomas A. Edison**

462. "Opportunity is missed by most people because it is dressed in overalls and looks like work." **Thomas A. Edison**

463. "We don't know a millionth of one percent about anything." **Thomas A. Edison**

464. "To invent, you need a good imagination and a pile of junk." **Thomas A. Edison**

465. "Results! Why man, I have gotten a lot of results. I know several thousand things that won't work." **Thomas A. Edison**

466. "All truths are easy to understand once they are discovered; the point is to discover them." **Galileo Galilei**

467. "I have never met a man so ignorant that I couldn't learn something from him." **Galileo Galilei**

468. "You cannot teach a man anything, you can only kelp him find it within himself." **Galileo Galilei**

469. "If I have seen farther than others, it is because I was standing on the shoulders of giants." **Isaac Newton**

470. "No great discovery was ever made without a bold guess." **Isaac Newton**

471. "I do not know what I may appear to the world, but to myself I seem to have been only like a boy playing on the seashore, and divesting myself now and then. Finding a smoother pebble or a pretties shell then ordinary, whilst the great ocean of truths lay all undiscovered before me." **Isaac Newton**

472. "A good compromise, a good piece of legislation, is like a good sentence; or a good piece of music. Everybody can recognize it. They say, 'huh. It work. It makes sense." **Barack Obama**

473. "Al Qaeda is still a threat. We cannot pretend somehow that because Barack Hussein Obama got elected as president, suddenly everything is going to be OK." **Barack Obama**

474. "America and Islam are not exclusive and need not be in competition, instead, they overlap, and share common principles of justice and progress, tolerance and the dignity of all human being." **Barack Obama**

475. "Americans; still believe in an America where anything's possible they just don't think their leaders do." **Barack Obama**

476. "Change will not come if we wait for some other person or some other time. We are the ones. We've been waiting for. We are the change that we seek." **Barack Obama**

477. "Focusing your life solely on making a buck shows a certain poverty of ambition. It asks too little of yourself. Because it's only when you hitch your wagon to something larger than yourself that you realize your true potential." **Barack Obama**

478. "I know my county has not perfected itself. At times, we've struggled to keep the promise of liberty and equality for all of our people. We've made our share of mistakes, and there are time when our actions around the world have not lived up to our best intentions." **Barack Obama**

479. "I think when you spread the wealth around it's good for everybody." **Barack Obama**

480. "If the people cannot trust their government to do the job for which it exists, to protect them and to promote their common welfare all else is lost." **Barack Obama**

481. "If you're walking down the right path and you're willing to keep walking eventually you'll make progress." **Barack Obama**

482. "It took a lot of blood, sweat and tears to get to where we are today, but we have just begun. Today we begin in earnest the work of making sure that the world we leave our children is just a little bit better then the one we inhabit today." **Barrack Obama**

483. "Serving God, through my works for others, make my life worth living." **Cleophus Jackson**

484. "Better a meal of vegetables where there is love than a fattened calf with hatred."

485. "It is easier for a camel to go through the eye of a needle, than for a rich man to enter the kingdom of God."

486. "Great men are not always wise."

487. "A fool shows his annoyance at once, but a prudent man overlooks an insult."

488. "Give, and it shall be given to you for whatever measure you deal out to others. It will be dealt to you in return."

489. "Nothing will benefit human health and increase the chances for survival of life on earth as much as the evolution to a vegetarian diet." **Albert Einstein**

490. "I have learned from an early age to abjured the use of meat, and the time will come when men such as I will look upon the murder of animals as they now look upon the murder of men." **Leonardo DA Vinci**

491. "Part of the secret of success in life is to eat what you like and let the food fight it out inside." **Mark Twain**

492. "Step up to God's thoughts." **Isaiah 55:9**

493. **"Without realizing it, God's word gets into our hearts for transformation and restoration." Romans 10:17**

494. "In the mouth of two or three witnesses may every word be established." **11 Corinthians 13:1**

495. "Where no counsel is, the people fall: but in the multitude of counselors there is safety." **Proverbs 11:14**

496. "Whatsoever thy hand finder to do, do it with thy might." Ecclesiastes **9:10**

497. "Do unto others as you would have others do unto you." **Matthew 7:20**

498. "As a man thinks in his heart, so is he." **Proverbs 23:7**

499. "There is that Speaker like the piercings of a sword; but the tongue of the wise is health." **Proverbs 12:18**

500. "Ask and it shall be given you; seek, and ye shall find; knock, and the door shall be opened." **Matthew 7:7**

501. "In the multitude of words there wantoner not sin; but he that refrain his lips is wise." **Proverbs 10:9**

502. "Love is patient; love is kind: love is not boastful or arrogant or rude. It does not insist on its own way; it is not irritable or resentful: it does not rejoice in wrongdoing. But rejoices in the truth. It bears all things. Believe all things, hopes all things, endures all things." **1 Corinthians 13:4-7**